Fresh Cut Flowers

Liz Schwartz & Stephen Seifert

Zippy Designs Publishing • Home of *The Foundation Piecer* • Newport, Virginia

Fresh Cut Flowers

Zippy Designs Publishing Inc.
RR 1 Box 187M
Newport, VA 24128
Phone:| 540.544.7153
Fax:| 540.544.7071
http://www.zippydesigns.com
ISBN 1-891497-07-3

Credits

Editor .... Liz Schwartz
Technical Editor ....Stephen Seifert
Book Designer .... Liz Schwartz
Quilting Assistant .... Robin Southern-Hypes

Acknowledgments

Thank you to Hoffman California Fabrics for supplying the batiks seen in the woodcut quilt and RJR Fashion Fabrics for their lovely line of quilter's sateens used in the floral quilt.

Introduction

While designing stained glass designs for a previous book, we noticed that by varying the thickness of the leading, an interesting woodcut look could easily be produced. As we kept trying new variations of this interesting effect, we soon had most of this stunning quilt designed.

While stitching the first blocks for the quilt, we found that you could make another entire quilt from the same floral blocks by removing the black woodcut areas creating a distinctively different look.

Printed in Korea
07 06 05 04 03 02   6 5 4 3 2 1

Contents

fresh cut flowers

Gathering
materials and supplies

Fabric

One of the benefits of foundation piecing is that it offers a great deal of flexibility in fabric selection. Fabrics that may be hard to handle when machine piecing such as silk, lamé, wool, and flannel become much easier to use when a foundation is used. The foundation helps to stabilize the material and prevent it from slipping and stretching. While we prefer to use mainly 100% cotton fabrics in our quilts, you can combine different types of fabric within a block to create interesting effects.

Nothing can be more heartbreaking than finding that after a quilt is finished one of the fabrics is not colorfast or shrinks. We always prewash our fabric before using it in a quilt. Use hot water when pre-washing and continue the process until the rinse water runs clear.

Foundation Materials

Paper is the preferred foundation material as it is readily available and inexpensive. Almost any type of paper can be used as a foundation. Before making all of the copies that you will need for a quilt, you should test the paper to make sure that it does not fall apart too quickly, or is tough to remove. Standard 20 lb. copier paper works well but can be hard to see through, so you need to have a good light source. We prefer to use a semi-transparent paper (*Easy Piece Foundation Paper*) so that the lines can easily be seen from both sides, making positioning fabric patches easier. Many quilters like to use freezer paper because the fabric patches adhere to the shiny side. Other suitable papers include typing paper, onion skin, vellum, tracing paper, and baking parchment.

In most cases, a removable foundation is desired unless you are using fragile fabrics and need extra stabilization. When fabric is used for a foundation it becomes a permanent part of the quilt, adding an extra layer may make hand quilting difficult. If you use a fabric foundation, choose a lightweight fabric in a neutral color.

Tools

- **Add-A-Quarter template ruler:** used for pre-trimming seams to a ¼".
- **Embroidery scissors:** a convenient size to keep near your sewing machine for trimming threads.
- **Flannel press cloth:** protects the iron, ironing board, and fabric from ink used in photocopiers and printers.
- **Iron and ironing board:** for setting seams and pressing pieces.
- **Postcard:** used with the Add-A-Quarter ruler to pre-trim fabric pieces.
- **Rotary cutter and mat:** needed to cut fabric strips and pre-trim the pieces while making the foundation units.
- **Rotary rulers (6" × 24" and 12½" × 12½"):** used with the rotary cutter and mat for cutting fabric strips and trimming foundation units.
- **Seam ripper:** choose one with a sharp point that can easily slip under tiny stitches.
- **Sewing machine:** any machine that has a straight stitch can be used to stitch the units.
- **Sewing thread:** use a sturdy 100% cotton in a neutral beige or gray for piecing the units.
- **Sewing pins:** flat flower head pins have long shanks and fine tips making them ideal for pin matching and holding fabrics in place.
- **Size 90/14 sewing machine needles:** a larger size needle helps to perforate the paper, making it easier to remove—change your needle each time you begin a new project.
- **Tweezers:** use a pair with serrated tips to help remove paper from tiny spots.
- **Vinyl-coated paper clips:** an invaluable tool for holding foundation sections when joining them together—the vinyl coating prevents rust spots on the fabric.
- **Wooden seam pressing bar:** helps to create flat, even seams.

*P*reparing
the foundations for sewing

*M*aking the Foundations

To use the patterns presented in this book, they must first be duplicated so they can be stitched. There are many methods that can be used to reproduce the foundations: needlepunching, photocopying, tracing, and scanning.

Needlepunching: This technique works best when many copies of the same block are needed; it is not especially suited to reproducing foundations for pictorial quilts. First, trace the pattern onto a piece of tracing paper. Layer the traced pattern with up to ten sheets of paper. Then, with an unthreaded sewing machine, sew along the lines.

Photocopying: Photocopying is the fastest and easiest way to make foundations for your project. For best results, we recommend that you test the accuracy of the machine before making all of your copies for the entire project. To do this, make a copy of the pattern on the machine. Place the copy over the original and hold it up to a light source. Look to see how closely the original matches the copy. If the copy is significantly different, choose another machine. To minimize distortion when copying, use the same machine to make all of the copies needed for the project at the same time.

Tracing: Although time consuming, tracing is an easy and accurate way to make copies that can be used with both fabric and paper foundations. Use a very fine mechanical pencil to carefully trace over the marked pattern lines.

Scanning: Lay the foundation master on the scanner bed, making sure that there are no stray objects or wrinkles which might cause gaps in the final scan. Choose a moderately high resolution—150 to 200 dpi to derive the most detail without overloading the computer with more information than is necessary. Once the image is scanned, you can print out as many copies as you like without going to the copy shop or spending the time to trace each foundation by hand.

After you have made all of the necessary foundations for the project, trim them out leaving about an 1/8" seam allowance around the dashed lines. To prepare the foundations for stitching, mark the colors in the spaces.

*C*hanging the Finished Size

When making copies of your foundations, it is easy to change the size of the finished block with a copy machine. Use the table below to determine the percentage to reduce or enlarge the foundations in order to achieve the desired size.

If you are making one of the featured quilts, make sure that you reduce or enlarge all of the parts needed for the quilt by the same percentages so that all of the parts will fit together when they are finished. You can also create some interesting variations by combining blocks of various sizes together in a quilt.

Block Reduction and Enlargement Chart		
Desired Size of Block	*Size of Block Quarter*	*Reduction or enlargement (% of original)*
18"	9"	150%
17"	8½"	142%
16"	8"	133%
15"	7½"	125%
14"	7"	117%
13"	6½"	108%
12"	6"	100%
11"	5½"	92%
10"	5"	83%
9"	4½"	75%
8"	4"	67%
7"	3½"	58%
6"	3"	50%
Reducing or enlarging the size of the finished block also changes the thickness of the black lines in the woodcut blocks.		

Understanding
foundation pieced patterns

Foundation Patterns

The drawn pattern, called a foundation, serves as the master plan on which your block will be built. Unlike traditional patchwork in which fabric patches are cut from templates and stitched together, foundation piecing eliminates the task of cutting templates and marking fabric, while allowing for a high degree of accuracy and control. Foundation patterns contain a set of "directions" built into the pattern that show how it is to be sewn. All solid lines marked on the pattern are sewing lines and the dashed line indicates where to trim the unit. The numbers on each of the pieces shows the order in which the fabric patches are added to the foundation unit.

It is important to note that when making the units you will do all of the sewing while looking at the printed side of the foundation and that the fabric patches will be placed on the reverse, or unprinted side of the foundation. The printed side of the foundation is the mirror image, or reverse, of the finished block (fabric side). Looking through the unprinted (blank) side of the paper will help to visualize the finished block. To avoid confusion when making the sections, look at the foundation from the unprinted side when envisioning fabric placement. The black leading areas are shaded in gray to aid in unit construction.

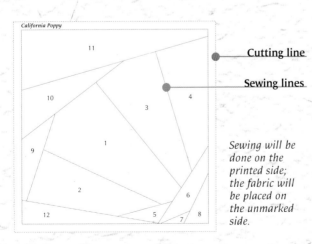

Sewing will be done on the printed side; the fabric will be placed on the unmarked side.

Cutting line

Sewing lines

Assembly Diagram

A visual map to block construction, the **Assembly Diagram** shows how the sections fit together to make the design. It is important to note that the **Assembly Diagram** shows the foundations from the printed side; the fabric side will be the mirror image of what is shown. Even though it may seem intuitive to flip the foundations over and look at the fabric side, all of the assembly steps are best done looking only at the printed side of the foundation.

 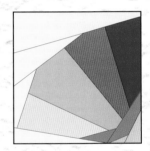

Foundation pattern (left) for ¼ of the California Poppy block and corresponding **Assembly Diagram** (right). Note the **Assembly Diagram** always shows the design as viewed from the printed side of the foundations. When marking foundations with colors, use the **Assembly Diagram** as a guide for color placement.

To assemble blocks that need multiple units for each block quarter, locate the lowercase letters in the seam allowances of the sections. Starting with a to a, match the lowercase letters and join the units alphabetically.

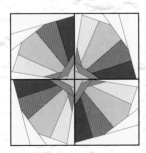 

Assembly Diagram (left) for the California Poppy block and photo (right). Since the right side of the fabric is placed on the unprinted side of the foundation, the finished block is the mirror image of both the pattern and **Assembly Diagram**.

*L*earning
the foundation piecing method

*C*utting Fabric Strips

Rather than cutting out the shape of the piece, as you would for traditional patchwork, we prefer to cut fabric strips and use them to piece the foundation sections. Using these strips helps to minimize fabric waste and keeps things organized.

When cutting strips for an entire quilt, start by locating the largest area where the fabric will be used and cutting the widest strips first. Leftover strips can be used for smaller areas, helping to avoid running short on fabric. If you are making a large quilt that requires many identical foundation units to complete, it is best to precut all of the pieces that you will need at the same time and stack them in piles at your work station. We find that this saves time when sewing the units and helps to avoid confusion and mistakes.

1 Starting with piece 1, measure the height and width of the area by placing a ruler over the section covered by the piece. Add at least a ½" seam allowance around each of the sides; the extra fabric will help to ensure that the fabric patch covers the area if it shifts during sewing.

Piece 1 measures 2L" x 4L". Including a generous H" seam allowance on each side, cut a 3L" wide strip of fabric. Then cut enough 5L" long pieces for all of the foundation units.

2 Cut a strip of fabric to the width of the measurement. Then cut a fabric patch from the strip to the length of the piece. Continue cutting pieces from the strip for all of the foundation sections needed for the quilt.

3 To measure for the next piece, lay the edge of the ruler along the seam line between pieces 1 and 2, so that it entirely covers piece 2. Look to see how large the piece is including a generous ½" seam allowance. Cut a strip of fabric to the width of the measurement and cut a fabric patch from the strip to the length needed. Cut enough pieces for all of the units. If needed, cut additional strips.

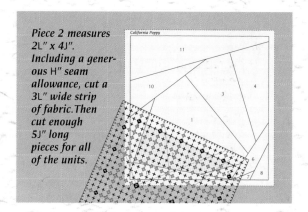

Piece 2 measures 2L" x 4J". Including a generous H" seam allowance, cut a 3L" wide strip of fabric. Then cut enough 5J" long pieces for all of the units.

4 Repeat the process described above to cut fabric pieces for all of the remaining pieces on the foundation section.

*F*abric Grain

When cutting fabric and piecing the foundation units, we do not usually concern ourselves with the grain of the fabric unless we are working with a directional print that will look awkward if it is not positioned on the straight of grain.

As long as your finished quilt is bordered by fabric that is cut from the straight of grain, you should not encounter any problems. We also highly recommend that you baste each of your finished sections within the ¼" seam allowance to prevent any distortion or stretching of the fabric when you are assembling the sections. When basting the foundations, use a very small stitch. The stitches do not need to be removed and will help to stabilize the edges and prevent them from fraying.

Directional Prints

Directional prints such as stripes and plaids may be used successfully in foundation piecing but look best when cut and pieced so that they are placed on the straight of grain.

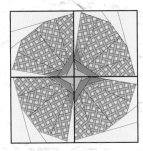 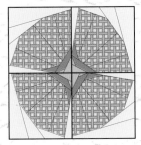

Using this technique to cut fabric pieces will allow you to use directional and one-way prints with ease. In situations where a directional print will be used, it is more visually appealing when the fabric patches are cut and pieced on the straight of grain (right), than when they are placed with a random grain pattern (left).

1 Rough cut a piece of fabric that covers the entire area plus seam allowances (in the example below, the directional fabric will be used in piece 3). When cutting the fabric, place it so the straight of grain is parallel to the edges of the foundation, and the print is positioned as it will be in the finished block. Place the foundation, with the printed side up, on top of the wrong side of the directional fabric (the directional fabric is placed right side down). Center the foundation over the fabric piece so that it covers the entire area of the piece to be added and check to see if it covers the entire area including a generous ½" seam allowance around all sides.

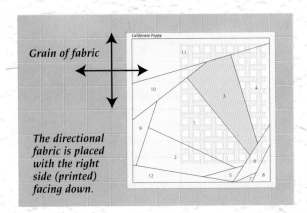

Grain of fabric

The directional fabric is placed with the right side (printed) facing down.

2 Place the edge of an index card on the line between the previous piece and the section in which the fabric will be used (in the example below, the card was placed on the line between pieces 1 and 3). Crease the foundation along the sewing line and fold it over the index card, towards the piece where the directional fabric will be used. Place an Add-A-Quarter ruler on top of the folded foundation and card, pushing the ¼" lip up against the fold.

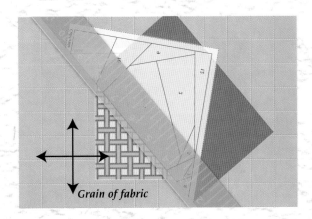

Grain of fabric

3 Using a rotary cutter, trim away the excess material. Using the cut piece as a template, trim enough pieces of fabric for the remaining foundation sections. Repeat this process for all of the areas in which the directional fabric will be used.

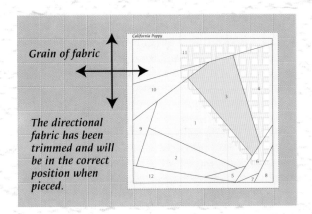

Grain of fabric

The directional fabric has been trimmed and will be in the correct position when pieced.

4 Piece the units in the usual manner; when you come to a piece where the directional fabric will be used, place the right side of the directional print down on top of the right side of the previous piece. Align the precut edge of the directional fabric with the pre-trimmed edge of the piece being added. Flip the unit to the printed side and stitch the seam.

Piecing the Units

After the pieces have been cut and the foundations are prepared, it is time to start sewing. The side of the foundation marked with the pattern lines and numbers is what you will be looking at when you are stitching the units; the fabrics will be placed on the unmarked (blank) side of the paper. Before you begin sewing, replace your needle with a size 90/14 and reduce your stitch length to 15–20 stitches per inch. While this technique can be used with either fabric or paper foundations, for the purposes of this discussion, we will be using a paper foundation.

1 Place your first piece of fabric right side up on the wrong (unprinted) side of the foundation. Holding the unit up to a light source (printed side of the foundation facing you), position the first piece of fabric. Make sure the fabric covers the entire area including a generous ¼" seam allowance. Pin the piece in place, or use a dab of glue from a glue stick.

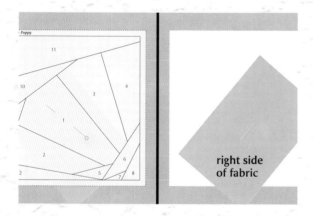

right side of fabric

2 Align a postcard along the sewing line between pieces 1 and 2. Crease the paper and fold it over the postcard (fold towards the piece with the lowest number) to reveal the excess fabric below.

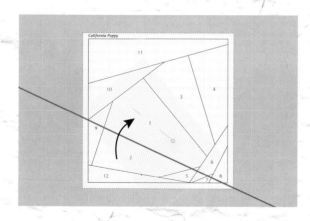

3 Place an Add-A-Quarter ruler on the crease and push the ¼" lip up against the fold. Using a rotary cutter, trim the excess fabric leaving a ¼" seam allowance.

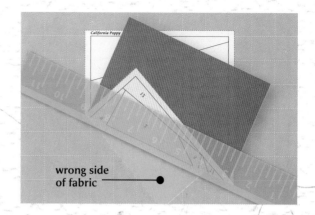

wrong side of fabric

4 Flip the unit to the unmarked side and align the next fabric patch, right side down, along the pre-trimmed edge. Looking through the paper from the printed side, check to see if the piece of fabric being added extends beyond the stitching line.

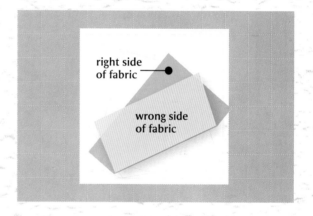

right side of fabric

wrong side of fabric

5 Flip the foundation (with the fabrics in place) to the printed side and sew on the line between the first and second pieces. Extend your line of stitching at least a ¼" before and after the printed line (this helps to prevent the seams from ripping out).

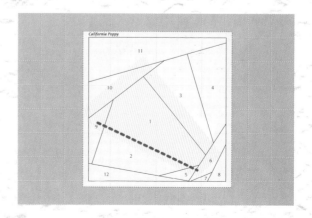

6 Place the foundation, with the printed side down, onto a flannel press cloth on the ironing board. Fold the fabric into place and gently press it with an iron. Holding the fabric firmly, press the seam with a wooden seam pressing bar to flatten the seam.

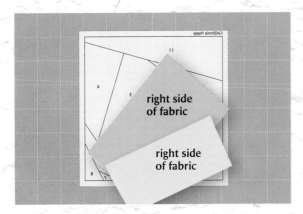

7 Place the postcard on the next sewing line (between pieces 1 and 3) and fold the paper over the postcard. If previous stitching prevents you from folding the foundation, carefully tear the paper away from those stitches so that it folds easily. Place an Add-A-Quarter ruler on the fold, and trim away the excess material, leaving a ¼" seam allowance.

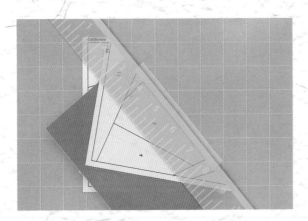

8 With right sides together, place the next piece of fabric on the blank side (fabric) of the foundation and align it with the pre-trimmed edge. Holding the unit up to a light source, check to see if the piece extends at least a ¼" past the sewing line.

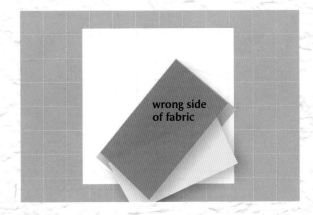

9 Flip the unit to the printed side and sew on the line between pieces 1 and 3. Continue pressing, trimming, and adding pieces until completed.

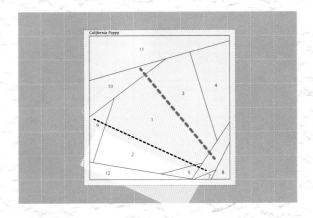

10 Using a very small stitch, baste around the entire foundation within the ¼" seam allowance. Be careful that the basting does not extend into the visible areas of the section (past the solid line).

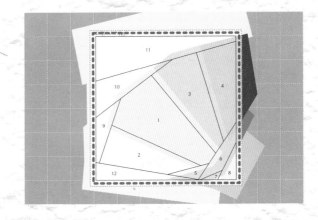

11 Trim the foundation along the outer (dashed) line, removing the excess fabric and paper from the section. Do not remove the paper from the blocks yet, as it helps to stabilize the fabric and aids in assembling the block.

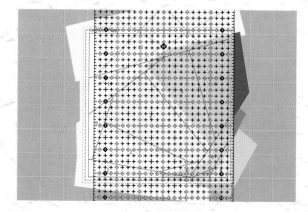

12 With the printed side facing you, arrange all of the units as shown in the **Assembly Diagram**. Turn the units to the fabric side and check to see if any mistakes were made while sewing the units.

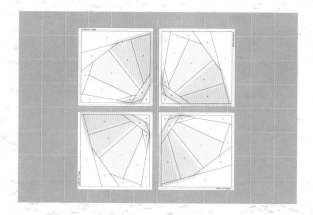

expert tip

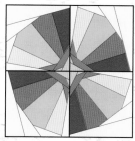

Assembly Diagram for the California Poppy block

The **Assembly Diagram** for each block is a visual map that depicts how the units fit together to make the block. While it may seem intuitive to flip the units to the fabric side and assemble them by looking at the photo of the finished block, you will find that assembling the units from the printed side is much easier and helps to prevent errors.

13 Identify several key points (such as corners, center seams, and obvious match points) and place pins through them so that the pin passes perpendicularly through the sewing lines (solid) on both foundations. When the sections are aligned, fasten them together using several vinyl-coated paper clips.

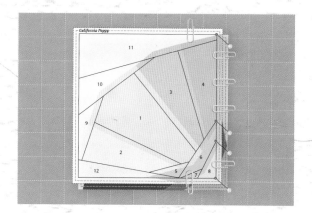

14 After the paper clips are set, remove all of the pins. Sew the units together, removing the paper clips as you sew. Be careful not to sew over the paper clips as they can damage your needle and cause the layers to shift.

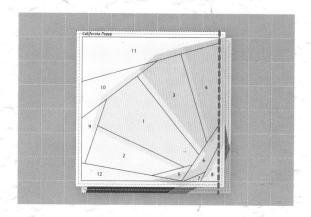

15 Carefully remove the paper only from the seam allowance area and press the seam open. Sew the remaining units together and join the halves to make the block.

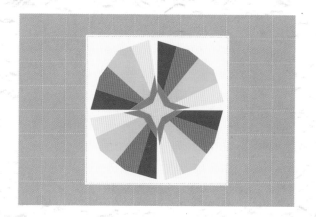

*F*inishing
techniques for your quilt

Basting

When the quilt top is completed, remove the paper foundations from the back of the quilt top (if you used a fabric foundation, it will not be removed). If you have trouble removing the paper, try using a pair of tweezers to get into tight spots. Lightly misting the paper with a sprayer will help to loosen it and make the paper easier to remove. To prepare your top for quilting, layer it with batting and backing, then baste the layers together.

1 Cut a piece of batting that is at least 1" larger on all sides than the quilt top. Then, cut a piece of backing fabric 1" larger than the batting. With the right side down, tape the backing down to a smooth flat surface.

2 Lay the batting on top of the backing. Center the quilt top on the batting; carefully smoothing out any wrinkles.

3 Starting in the center of the quilt, baste the entire surface of the quilt top, leaving no more than a 4" space between the lines. To baste with thread, use a long darning needle (or doll making needle) and work outward from the center in a grid pattern (avoid dark colored threads as they may leave dye behind in the fabric). Alternatively, you can use safety pins to hold the layers together.

Quilting

Since foundation pieced quilts often have many seams, some areas of the quilt top may become very thick, making hand quilting difficult. Most of the projects in this book are best quilted by machine. Hand quilted motifs may be added to the border, or any large open space in the project. There are two main approaches that can be taken to quilting your project: using a walking foot for straight lines, and "in the ditch" quilting, or free-motion quilting.

Even Feed Quilting | By using a walking foot to help the layers move through the machine evenly, you can create many interesting patterns with straight or gently curving lines. One of the easiest ways to quilt a project is to outline each of the seams, or "quilt in the ditch". Another basic technique is echo quilting, in which a series of lines echoing the shape of the piece are quilted at set intervals. Free-form patterns which do not contain any sharply curving sections can also be quilted with a walking foot.

Free-motion Quilting | Any number of patterns can be created by lowering the feed dogs of the sewing machine, using a free motion quilting foot, and hand guiding the quilt sandwich. A meandering stitch can be used to fill large areas of background. You can also create spirals, stars, circles, as well as numerous other fill designs. This type of quilting usually requires a bit more practice than even feed quilting, but it allows for almost unlimited creativity.

While there is a wide variety of batting in both natural and synthetic fibers available, we find that we prefer to use 100% cotton almost exclusively as it lends a soft, old-fashioned feeling to the quilt. Wool batting also adds a cozy touch with the added benefit of being very warm in the winter. However, if you plan to hand quilt, cotton batting can be tough to stitch through and you may want to consider using polyester batting. If your quilt uses large amounts of black or dark colors, use a black or gray batting.

Adding a Hanging Sleeve

To make displaying your quilts easier, make a hanging sleeve and attach it to the back of your quilt before the binding is attached.

1 Measure the width of your quilt and subtract 2" from the measurement. Cut a 6"–9" (double the width of the desired size of the finished sleeve) wide strip of fabric to the length needed. If necessary, piece strips together until it is the right length.

2 Turn each of the ends under a ¼". Turn the ends under another ¼" and edge stitch along the inner fold to make a hem with a finished edge.

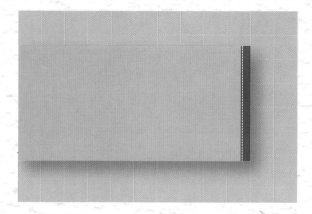

3 Fold the strip in half lengthwise, with wrong sides together, aligning the raw edges. Press the fold. Using an ⅛" seam allowance, stitch the raw edges together to form a tube. Align the raw edge of the tube with the raw edge of the quilt top and pin the sleeve in place. Using a scant ¼" seam allowance, baste the sleeve in place. The quilt is now ready for binding.

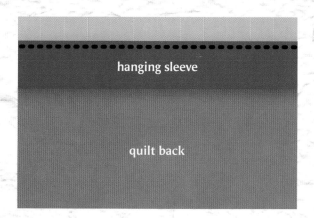

hanging sleeve

quilt back

Binding

We like to use binding strips cut from the straight of grain. If your quilt will receive heavy wear or will be used on a bed, consider using a bias binding for added strength and durability.

To prepare your quilt for binding, baste around the perimeter of the quilt, using an ⅛" seam allowance (the basting will be covered by the binding). Trim away the excess batting and backing and square up the corners of your quilt. Remove any remaining basting stitches and loose threads.

Making the Binding

1 Measure the total length of all sides of the quilt and add an extra 16" to that measurement (fabric allowance for corners and joining). Cut enough 2½"-wide strips from the crosswise grain (or bias grain, if desired) of the binding fabric to equal the measurement.

2 With right sides together, join the strips together using a diagonal seam to make a continuous strip.

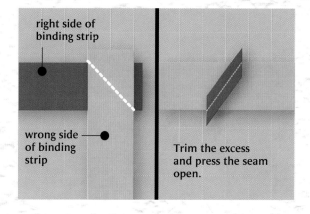

right side of binding strip

wrong side of binding strip

Trim the excess and press the seam open.

3 Fold the strip in half lengthwise with the wrong sides together, aligning the cut edges, and press.

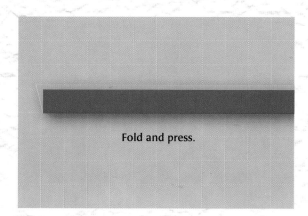

Fold and press.

Attaching the Binding

1 Starting at the bottom of the quilt, align the raw edges of the binding and quilt. Using a walking foot, begin stitching, leaving an 8"–10" tail of binding. Continue until you are ¼" away from a corner.

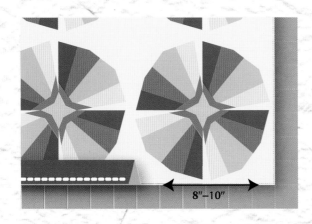

2 At the ¼" point, stop sewing and back stitch. Remove the quilt from the sewing machine. Fold the binding straight up from the corner creating a 45° angle.

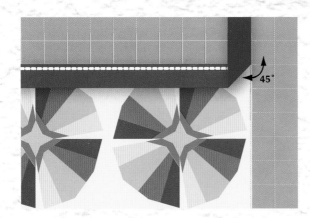

3 While holding the crease in place, fold the binding strip down so that the raw edge is aligned with the edge of the quilt, and continue sewing from the top of the corner.

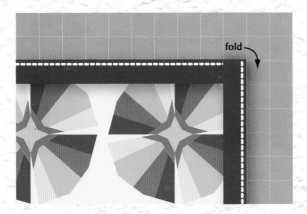

4 Continue attaching the binding until you are about 8" from the starting point. To join the ends, overlap the end of the binding strip 2½" and trim the excess.

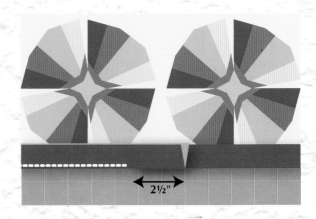

5 Open the strips and with right sides together, align the edges at right angles. Using a diagonal seam, join the strips. Trim the excess and press the seam open.

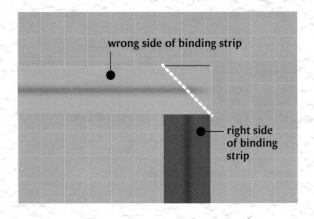

6 Fold the binding back in place and finish sewing the binding. Fold the binding over the raw edge of the quilt and blind stitch the edge in place.

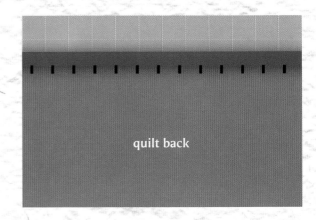

Labeling your Quilt

Preserve the history of your quilt for generations to come by finishing it with a fabric label.

1 Cut a patch of fabric that is ½" larger on all sides than the desired size of the finished label.

2 Turn the sides under a ¼" and press the fold with an iron. Fold the side edges under another ¼", creating a finished edge, and top stitch the seam in place. Repeat this process with the top and bottom edges.

back of label

3 Using a permanent fabric pen, record all of the information on the label. It is a good idea to include your name, place where the quilt was made, year, design used, and the source of the pattern, name of the recipient, and occasion for which the quilt was made (if applicable). If you have a sewing machine that can sew letters and numbers, you may wish to embroider these details, instead of using a fabric pen. You could even use a few extra blocks and piece them onto the label to give it a nicer appearance.

4 Position the label on the quilt and hand appliqué it in place.

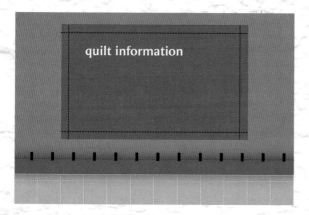

quilt information

expert tips

* To create an interesting kaleidoscope effect, use the technique for directional fabrics. Instead of placing the piece on the straight of grain, be sure to center the design motif in the piece as you want it to appear when finished. Then, cut it as you would a directional fabric.

* When adding a piece which forms an acute angle with the previous piece, extend your line of stitching at least ½" past the printed sewing line so that you will have enough fabric to maintain a ¼" seam allowance.

* If you make a mistake and need to replace a piece of fabric, gently remove the stitches with a seam ripper; then remove the piece of fabric and resew the seam. A ripped foundation can easily be repaired with a little transparent tape. However, if you sew over the tape it leaves a sticky residue on the needle.

* When sewing a triangular shaped piece that comes to a sharp point at one end, always start stitching at the widest end and sew towards the point. This helps to keep the points sharp.

* Ideally, your line of stitching should always be exactly on the printed lines. If your stitching wanders off occasionally it will usually not show in the middle of the seam; the beginning and ending points of the line are the most critical.

* If you find that when you join your blocks the points are not matching quite as well as you expected, check to see that the seams are pressed properly. If you see little tucks in your pieces, it is an indication that you need to spread the seam open more while you are pressing.

* When joining your foundation sections, always press the seam open to eliminate bulkiness. To stabilize the seam, double stitch each of the seams. After the sections are joined, open the piece and check it, then sew another seam on top of the original line of stitching.

Fresh Cut Flowers
floral quilt

Materials

Quilt Size: 84" x 102"

4¾ yds. light tan (background for leaves and center medallion)

7¼ yds. medium tan (background for flower blocks and Border section C)

1 yd. rust floral print (border section C)

1¼ yds. medium green (leaves)

1½ yds. dark green (leaves)

Fabric	Block(s)	Fabric	Block(s)
½ yd. light mauve	California Poppy, Hosta, Rose	¼ yd. light green	Clematis, Poinsettia
1 yd. medium mauve	California Poppy, Crocus, Chrysanthemum, Hosta, Magnolia, Rose, Zinnia	¾ yd. medium green	Anemone, California Poppy, Chrysanthemum, Clematis, Lily of the Valley, Zinnia
½ yd. dark mauve	California Poppy, Chrysanthemum, Magnolia, Rose, Zinnia	½ yd. dark green	California Poppy, Dahlia, Passion Flower
1½ yds. light magenta	California Poppy, Cosmos, Hosta, Passion Flower, Phlox, Plumeria, Poinsettia	½ yd. light blue	Hydrangea, Japanese Iris
		½ yd. medium blue	Anemone, Clematis, Japanese Iris, Cactus Flower
¾ yd. medium magenta	Cactus Flower, Phlox, Center Medallion	½ yd. dark blue	Aster, Clematis, Japanese Iris
¾ yd. dark magenta	Cactus Flower, Impatiens, Passion Flower, Plumeria, Poinsettia	¼ yd. light purple	Aster, Campanula
		¼ yd. medium purple	Anemone, Campanula
½ yd. medium red	Cosmos, Daffodil, Geranium	½ yd. light brown	Aster
¼ yd. dark red	Dahlia		
¼ yd. light orange	Campanula	¼ yd. medium brown	Aster, Sunflower
½ yd. medium orange	Daffodil, Dahlia, Geranium	½ yd. dark brown	Aster, Black Eyed Susan, Dogwood Blossom, Sunflower
½ yd. light yellow	Black Eyed Susan, Crocus, Impatiens, Marigold		
½ yd. medium yellow	Black Eyed Susan, Chrysanthemum, Daffodil, Geranium, Marigold, Rose, Sunflower, Medallion	1¼ yds. white	Crocus, Dogwood Blossom, Hosta, Lily of the Valley, Magnolia, Marigold
Border sections A and B are made using randomly placed scraps from the fabrics used in the blocks			

Making the Quilt Top

1 Make one each of the following blocks: Anemone, Aster, Black Eyed Susan, Cactus Flower, California Poppy, Campanula, Chrysanthemum, Clematis, Cosmos, Crocus, Daffodil, Dahlia, Dogwood Blossom, Geranium, Hosta, Hydrangea, Impatiens, Japanese Iris, Lily of the Valley, Magnolia, Marigold, Passion Flower, Phlox, Plumeria, Poinsettia, Rose, Sunflower, Zinnia, and the Center Medallion.

2 Using the medium green, dark green, and light tan fabrics, make 40 each of Leaf sections A and B. Do not assemble these subunits into blocks yet, they need to be joined in a specific way to construct the quilt.

3 Using the rust floral print and medium tan fabrics, make 36 of Border section C.

4 Using the scraps left over from piecing the blocks, make 14 of Border section A and 16 of Border unit B. Place the colors within each section randomly.

5 Flip all of the completed blocks and units to the printed side (fabric side down) and arrange them as shown in the **Quilt Assembly Diagram** (see page 19).

6 Starting at the center of the quilt, construct the 2 short diagonal rows that attach to the sides of the medallion. Referring to the **Quilt Assembly Diagram,** join the sections and attach them to the medallion.

7 Stitch the remaining six diagonal rows that comprise the inner portion of the quilt top and join them to the center medallion.

8 Make 2 inner side border strips, each containing 8 of Border section B. Add these strips to the left and right sides of the quilt top. Make the remaining 2 inner border strips using 7 Border A sections per strip; stitch these strips to the top and bottom edges.

9 Using the remaining blocks and border sections, make the side border strips. Stitch these strips to the left and right sides of the quilt top. Join the blocks and sections to make the upper and lower border strips and add these strips to the top and bottom edges.

Finishing the Quilt

1 Remove the paper from the back of the quilt top. If you have trouble removing the paper from tight areas, use a pair of tweezers to help reach into tough spots.

2 Layer the quilt top with batting and backing. Baste the layers together.

3 Machine quilt "in the ditch" around each of the flowers and leaves to hold the layers in place. Stipple the light tan background areas in the center of the quilt surrounding the leaves and medallion. Free-motion quilt a leaf design in the inner border and add softly curving lines in the petals of the flowers and center medallion. Quilt floral designs in the center of the outer border blocks

4 Embellish the flowers with beads, decorative quilting with metallic thread, or embroidery to add an extra dimension to your quilt.

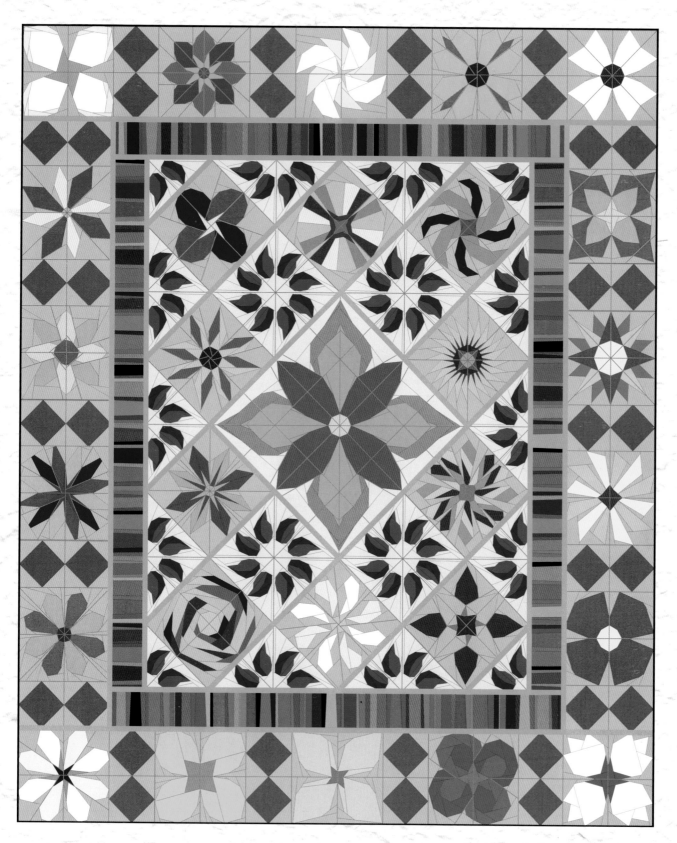

Quilt Assembly Diagram
(view from marked side of foundations)

*A*nemone

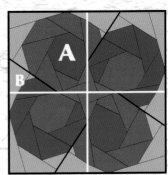

ake 4 each of sections A and B. Matching the lower case letters in the seam allowances, join the sections to make 4 quarters. Stitch the A/B sections together to make the block.

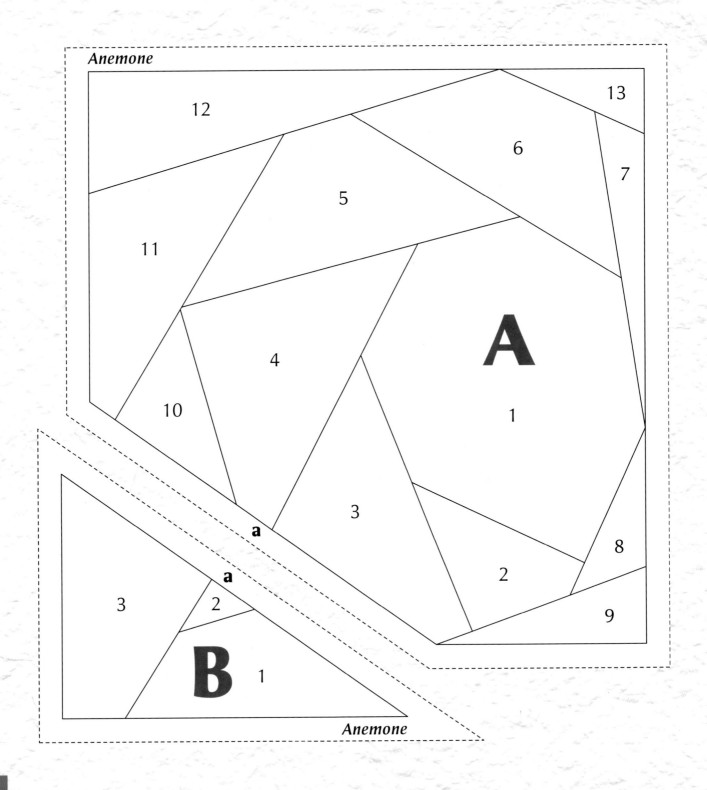

*A*ster

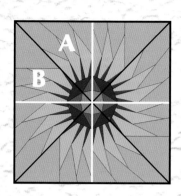

Make 4 each of sections A and B. Matching the lower case letters in the seam allowances, join the sections to make 4 quarters. Stitch the A/B sections together to make the block.

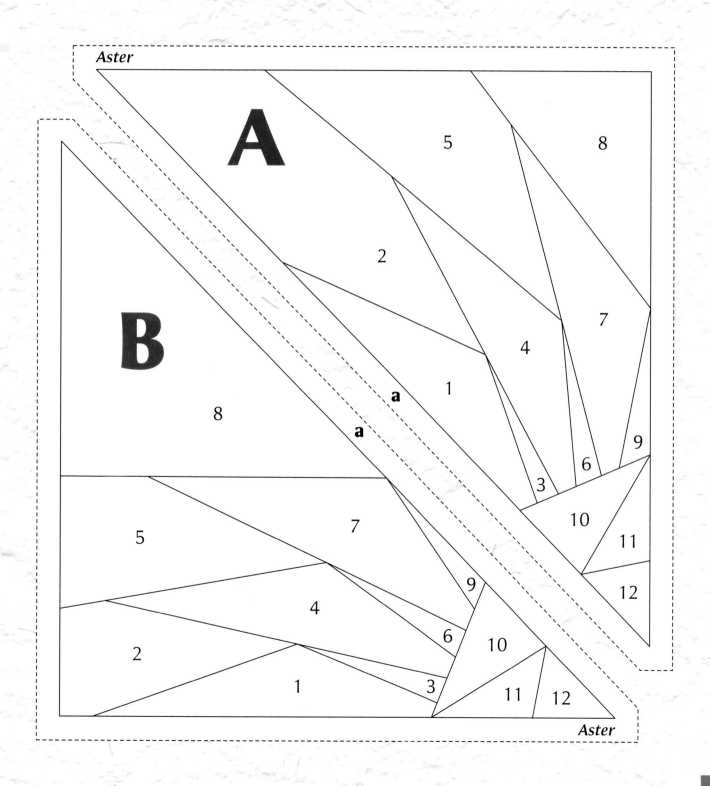

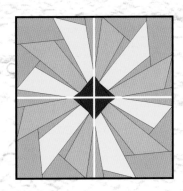

Black Eyed Susan

Make 4 of the foundation unit. Join the sections to make the block.

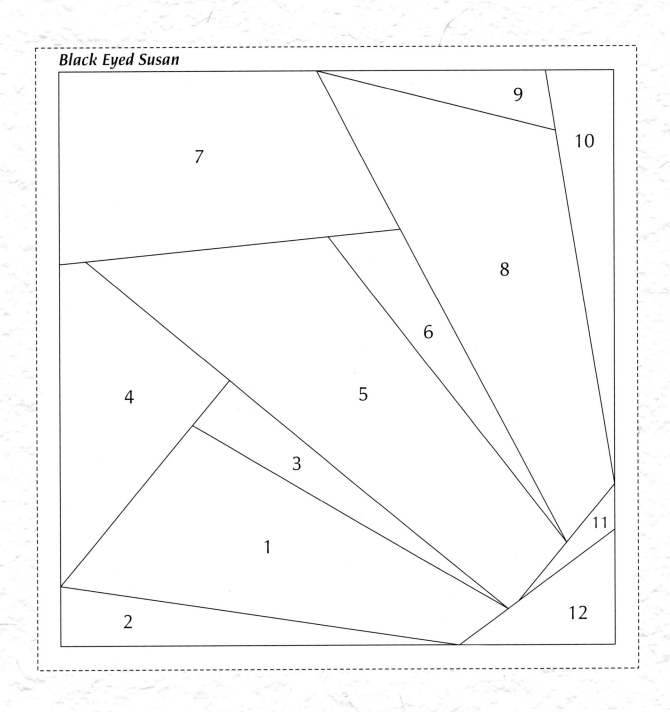

Black Eyed Susan

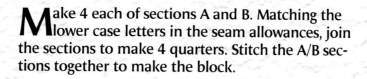

Cactus Flower

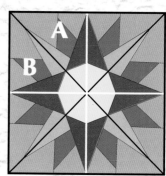

Make 4 each of sections A and B. Matching the lower case letters in the seam allowances, join the sections to make 4 quarters. Stitch the A/B sections together to make the block.

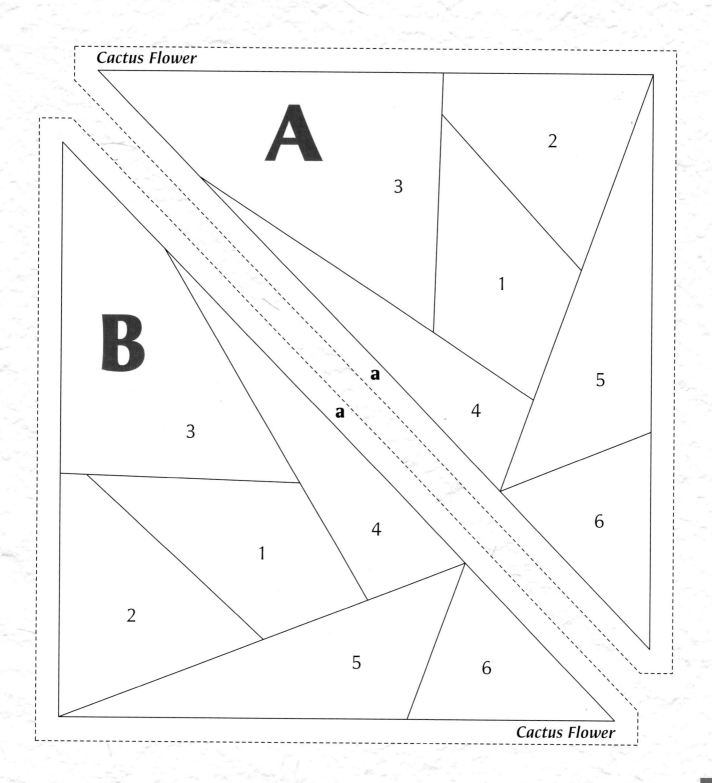

Cactus Flower

A

2

3

1

5

4

a

a

B

3

4

5

6

1

2

5

6

Cactus Flower

California Poppy

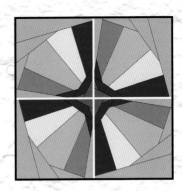

Make 4 of the foundation unit. Join the sections to make the block.

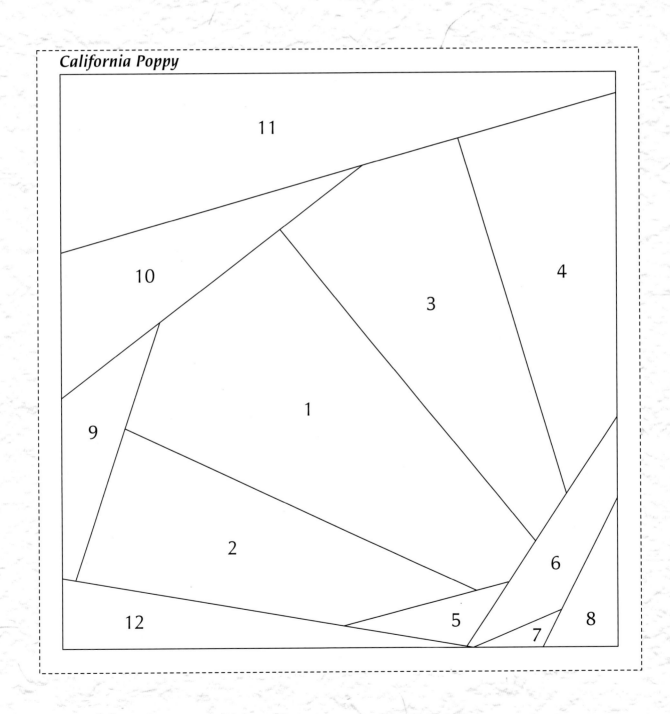

California Poppy

11

10

4

3

1

9

2

6

12

5

8

7

Campanula

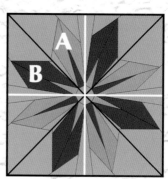

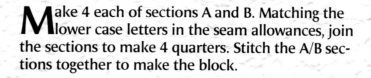

M ake 4 each of sections A and B. Matching the lower case letters in the seam allowances, join the sections to make 4 quarters. Stitch the A/B sections together to make the block.

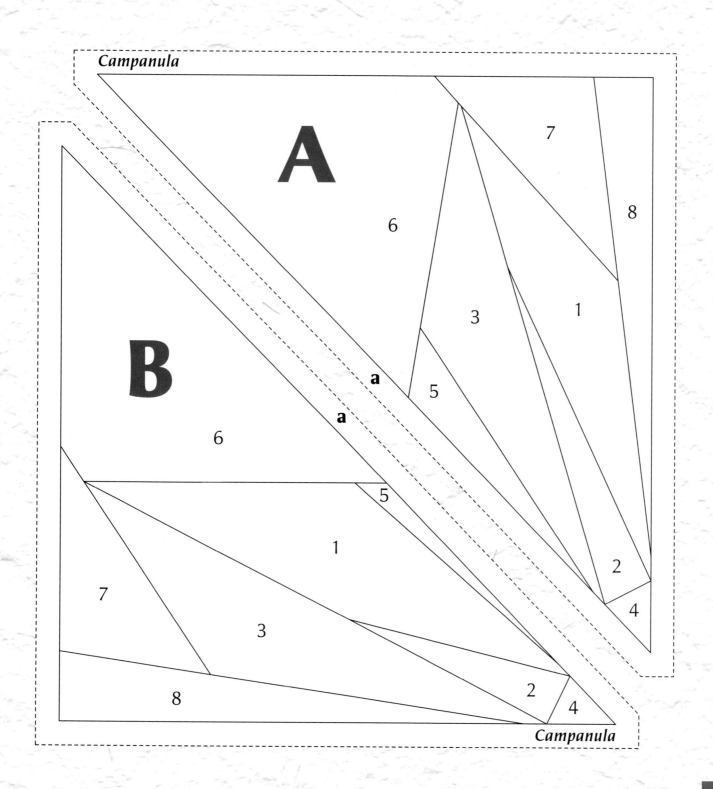

Campanula

A

6

7

8

3

5

1

a

a

2

4

B

6

5

1

7

3

2

8

4

Campanula

Chrysanthemum

Make 4 each of sections A—C. Matching the lower case letters in the seam allowances, join the sections to make 4 quarters. Stitch the A/B/C sections together to make the block.

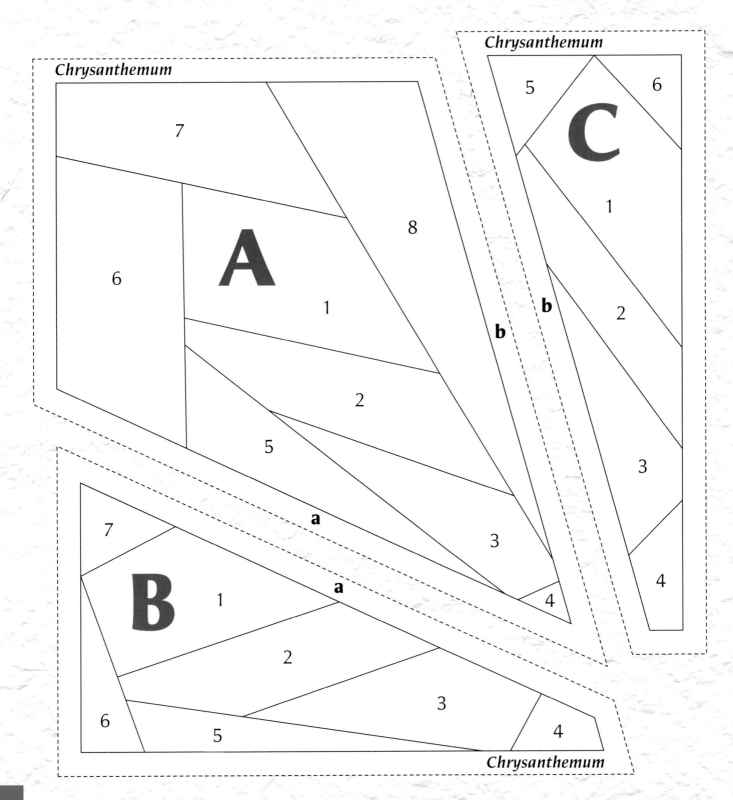

Chrysanthemum

7

6

A

1

8

2

5

a

B

7

1

a

2

6

5

3

4

Chrysanthemum

Chrysanthemum

5

6

C

1

b

b

2

3

3

4

4

*C*lematis

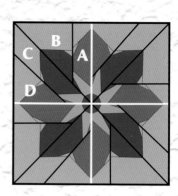

Make 4 each of sections A—D. Matching the lower case letters in the seam allowances, join the sections to make 4 quarters. Stitch the A/B/C/D sections together to make the block.

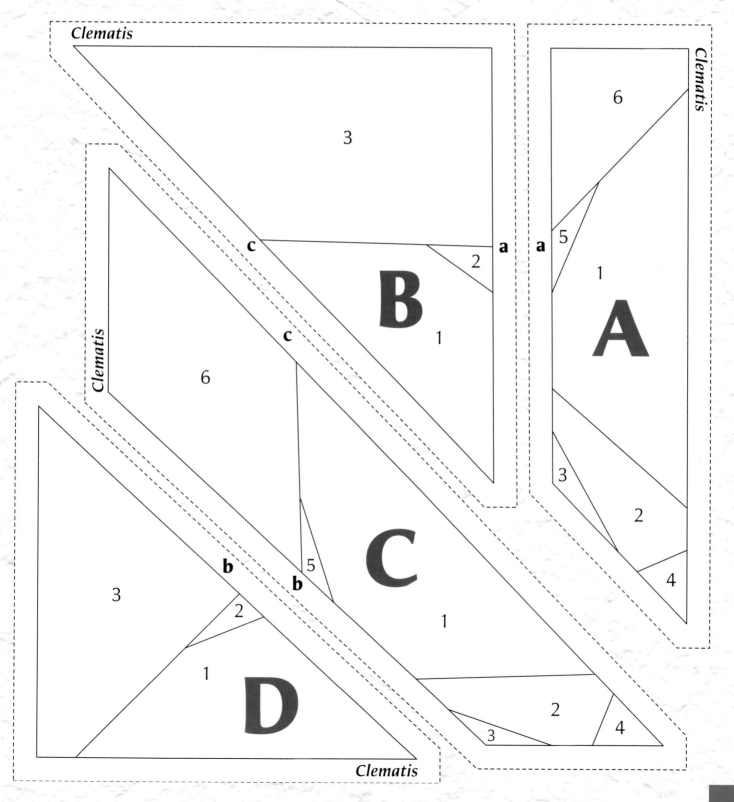

Clematis

Clematis

Clematis

3

c

c

B

1

2

a

6

a

5

1

A

3

2

4

Clematis

6

b

b

5

C

1

3

2

1

D

2

3

4

Clematis

Cosmos

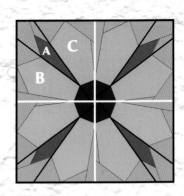

Make 4 each of sections A—C. Matching the lower case letters in the seam allowances, join the sections to make 4 quarters. Stitch the A/B/C sections together to make the block.

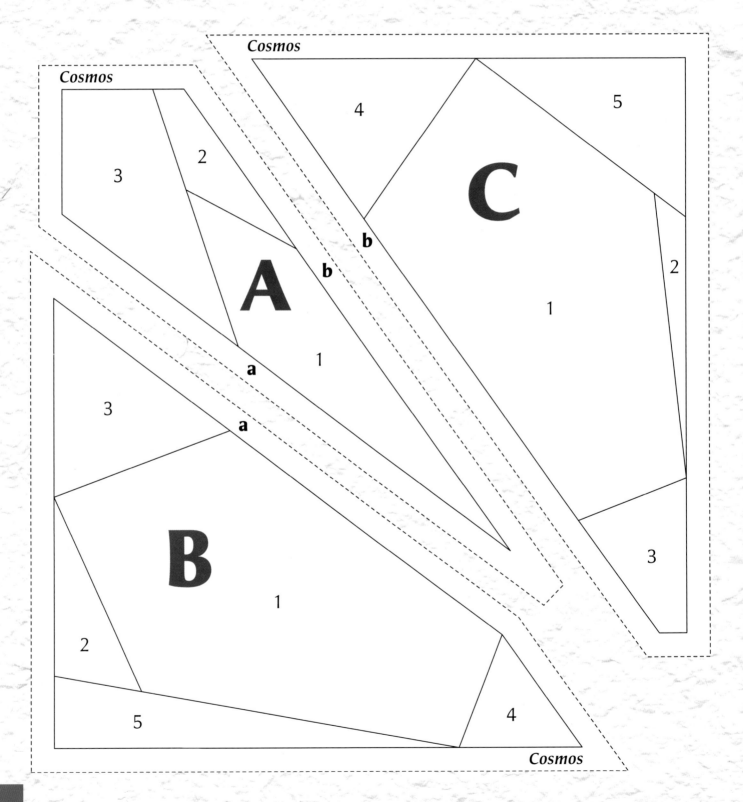

Crocus

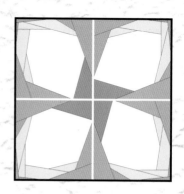

Make 4 of the foundation unit. Join the sections to make the block.

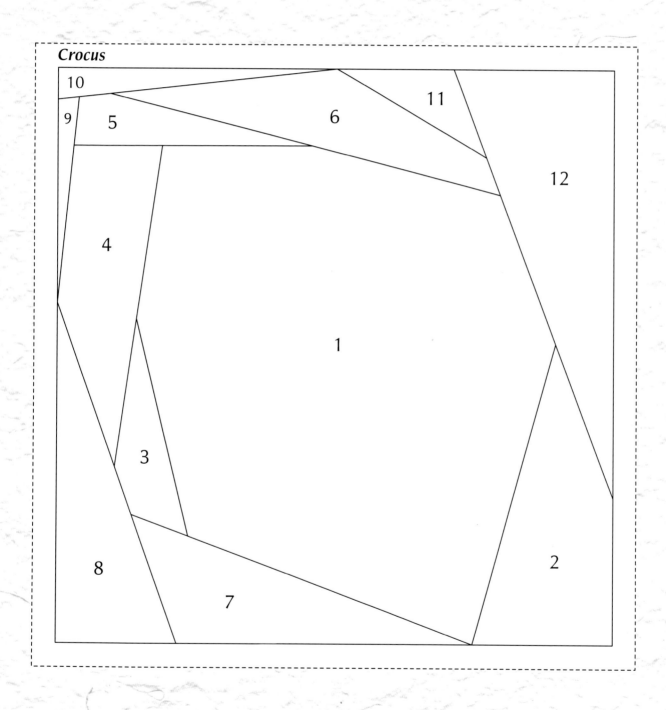

Crocus

Daffodil

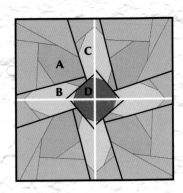

Make 4 each of sections A—D. Matching the lower case letters in the seam allowances, join the sections to make 4 quarters. Stitch the A/B/C/D sections together to make the block.

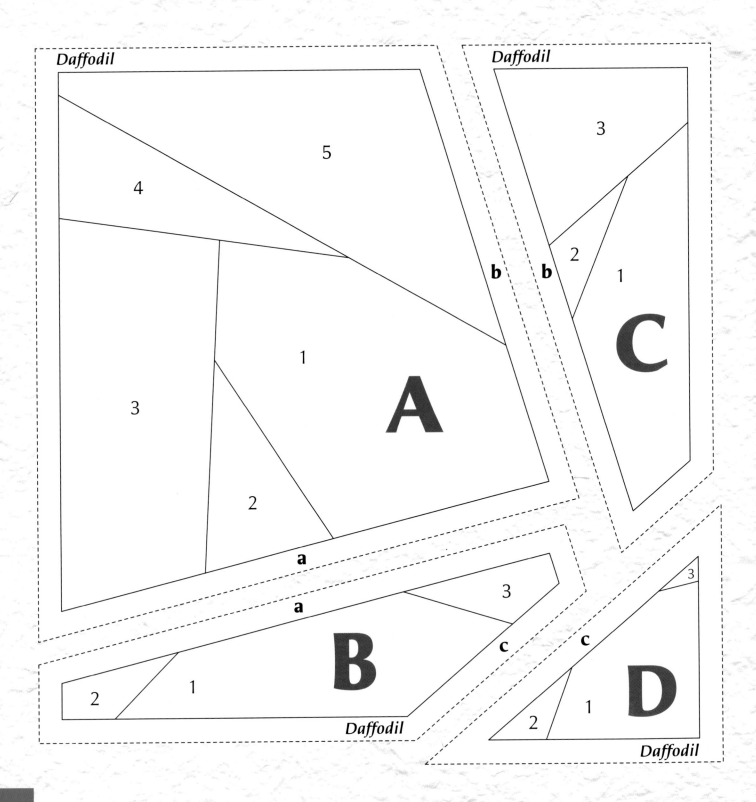

Daffodil

5

4

3

1

2

3

A

Daffodil

3

b b

2

1

C

a

a

3

B

c c

2 1

3

D

1

2

Daffodil

Daffodil

Dahlia

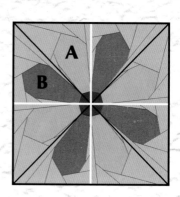

Make 4 each of sections A and B. Matching the lower case letters in the seam allowances, join the sections to make 4 quarters. Stitch the A/B sections together to make the block.

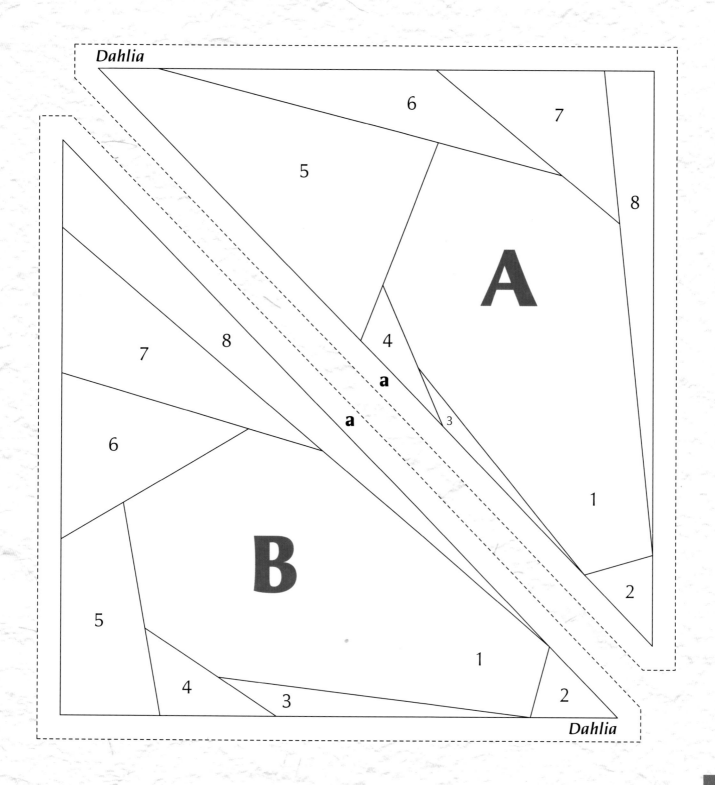

Dahlia

6

7

5

8

A

4

a

a

3

8

7

6

1

B

2

5

1

4

3

2

Dahlia

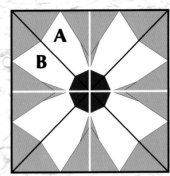

Dogwood Blossom

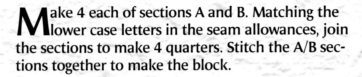

Make 4 each of sections A and B. Matching the lower case letters in the seam allowances, join the sections to make 4 quarters. Stitch the A/B sections together to make the block.

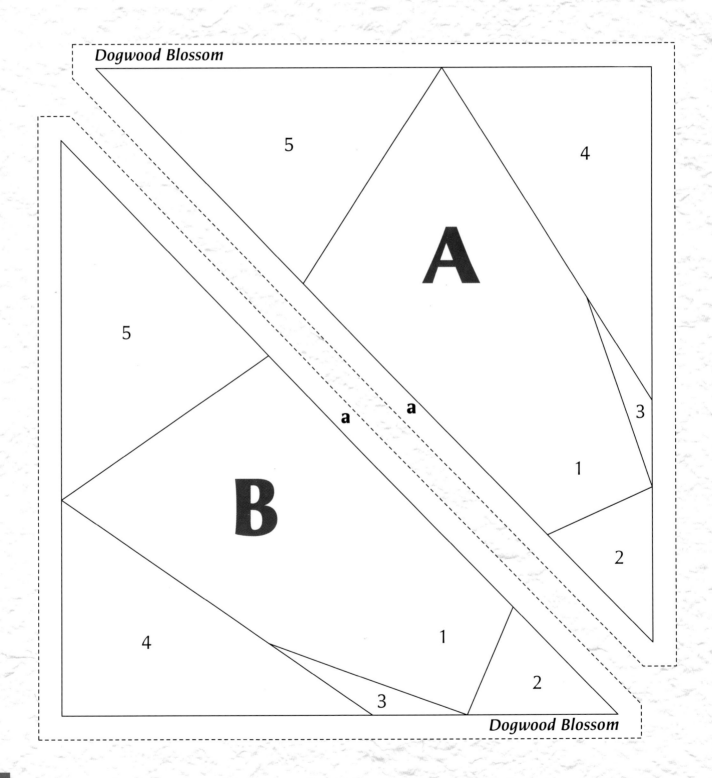

Dogwood Blossom

5

4

A

5

3

1

a   a

B

2

4

1

2

3

Dogwood Blossom

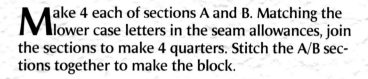

Geranium

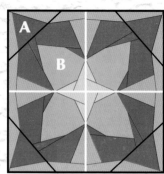

Make 4 each of sections A and B. Matching the lower case letters in the seam allowances, join the sections to make 4 quarters. Stitch the A/B sections together to make the block.

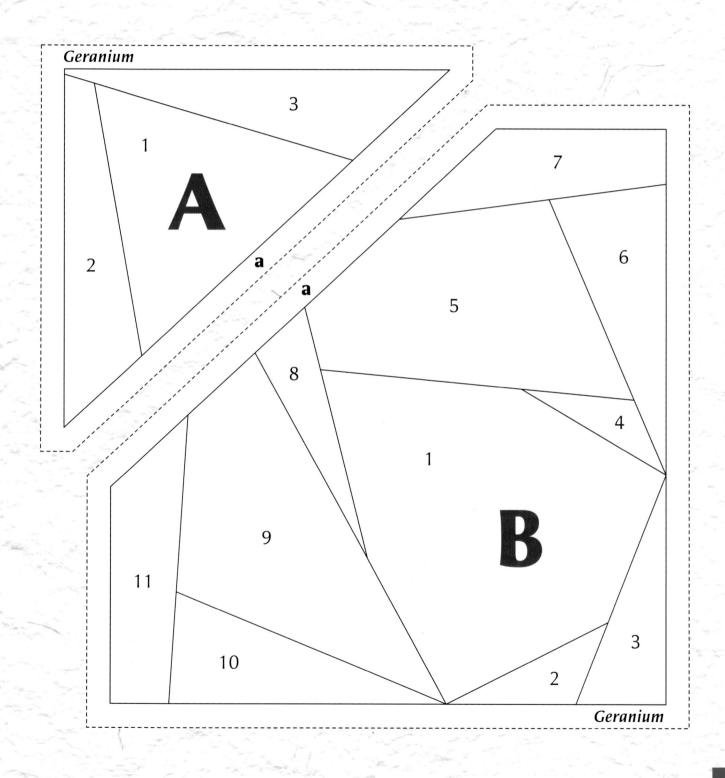

Geranium

A

1

3

2

a

a

7

6

5

8

4

1

B

9

11

10

3

2

Geranium

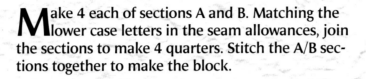

*H*osta

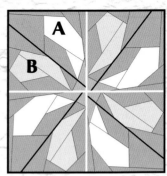

Make 4 each of sections A and B. Matching the lower case letters in the seam allowances, join the sections to make 4 quarters. Stitch the A/B sections together to make the block.

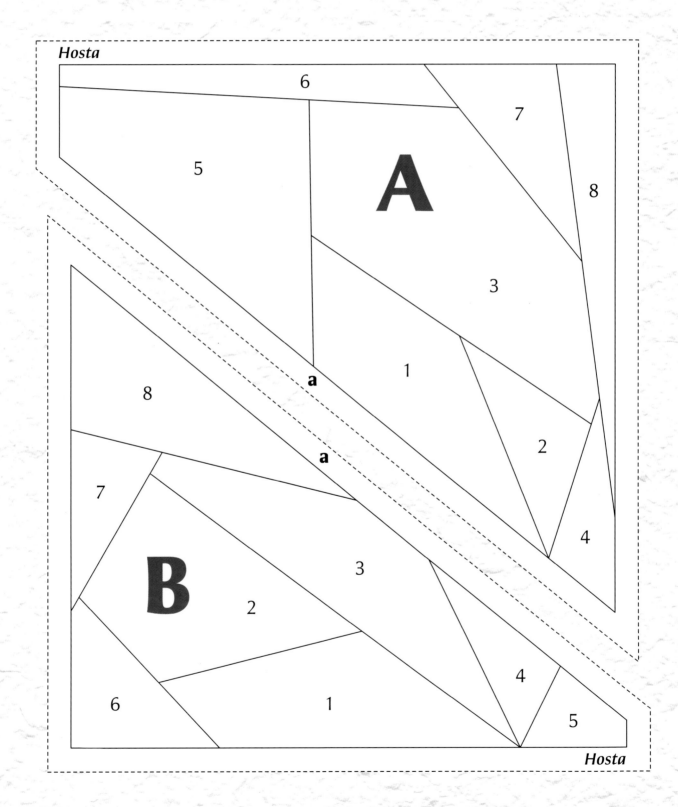

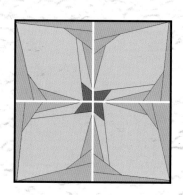

*H*ydrangea

Make 4 of the foundation unit. Join the sections to make the block.

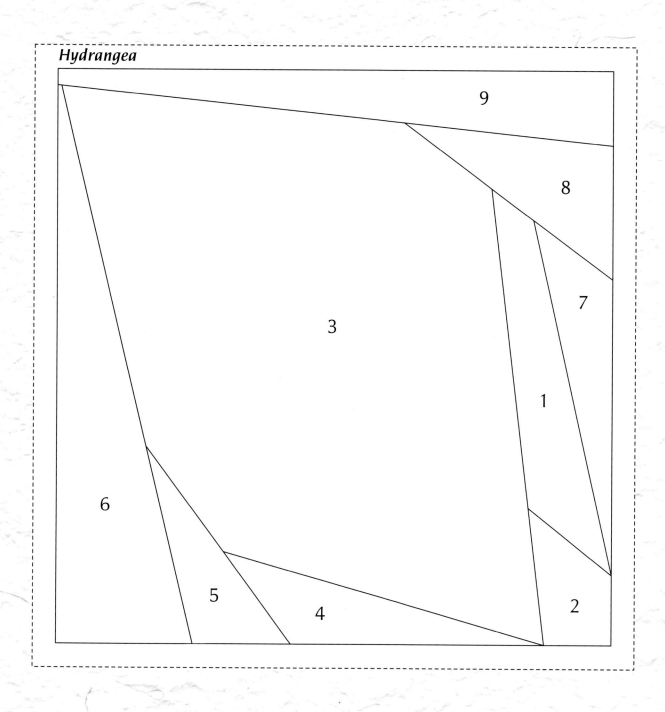

Hydrangea

9

8

7

3

1

6

2

5

4

Impatiens

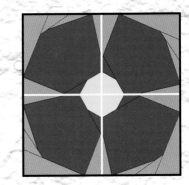

Make 4 of the foundation unit. Join the sections to make the block.

Impatiens

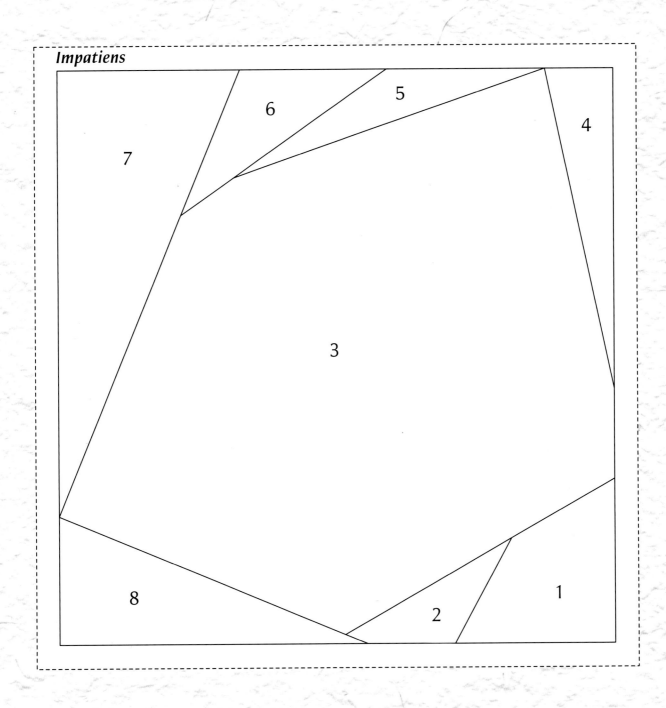

7

6

5

4

3

8

2

1

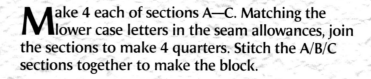

Japanese Iris

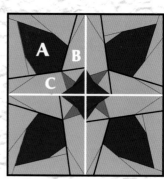

Make 4 each of sections A—C. Matching the lower case letters in the seam allowances, join the sections to make 4 quarters. Stitch the A/B/C sections together to make the block.

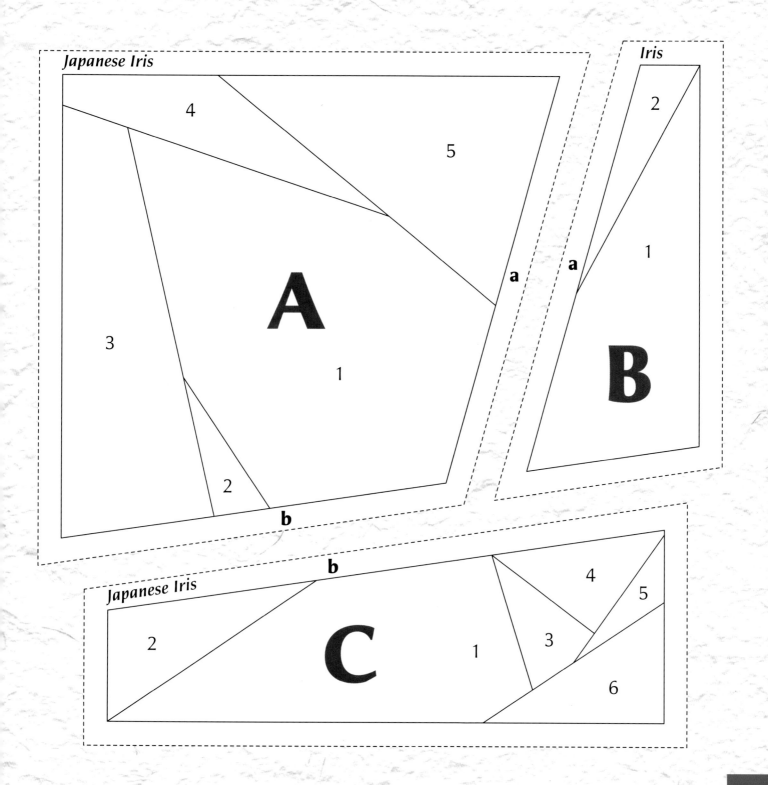

Japanese Iris

4

5

3

A

1

2

a

a

1

b

Iris

2

1

B

b

Japanese Iris

2

C

1

3

4

5

6

Lily of the Valley

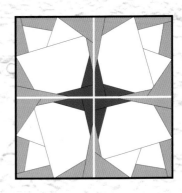

Make 4 of the foundation unit. Join the sections to make the block.

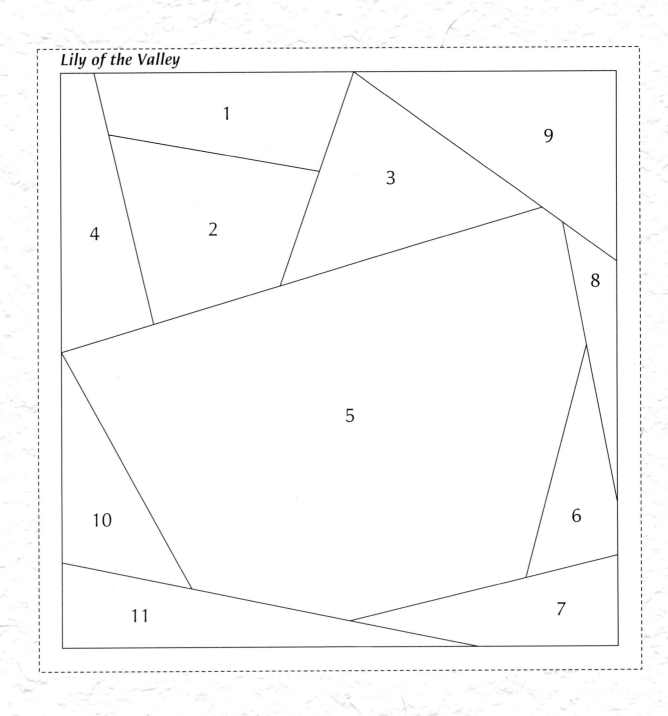

Lily of the Valley

1

9

3

4

2

8

5

10

6

7

11

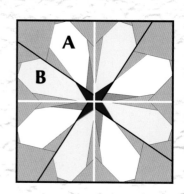

*M*agnolia

*M*ake 4 each of sections A and B. Matching the lower case letters in the seam allowances, join the sections to make 4 quarters. Stitch the A/B sections together to make the block.

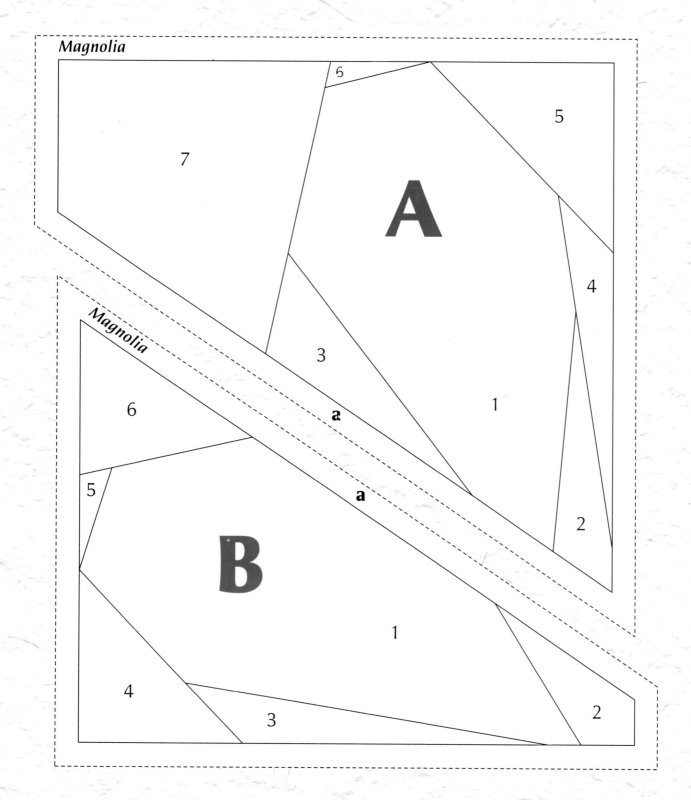

Magnolia

6

5

7

A

4

3

a

1

a

Magnolia

6

5

B

2

1

4

3

2

Marigold

Make 4 of the foundation unit. Join the sections to make the block.

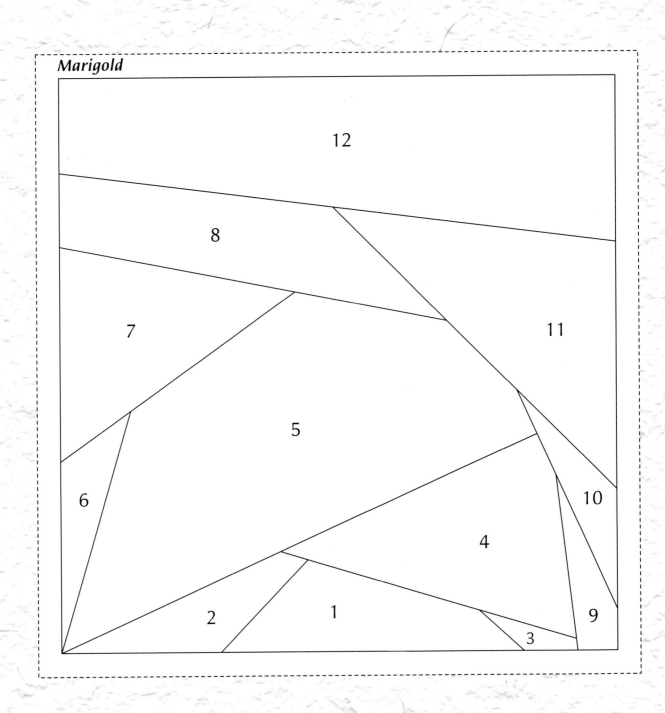

Marigold

12

8

7

11

5

6

10

4

2

1

9

3

*P*assion Flower

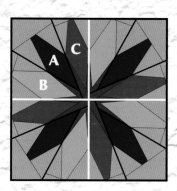

Make 4 each of sections A—C. Matching the lower case letters in the seam allowances, join the sections to make 4 quarters. Stitch the A/B/C sections together to make the block.

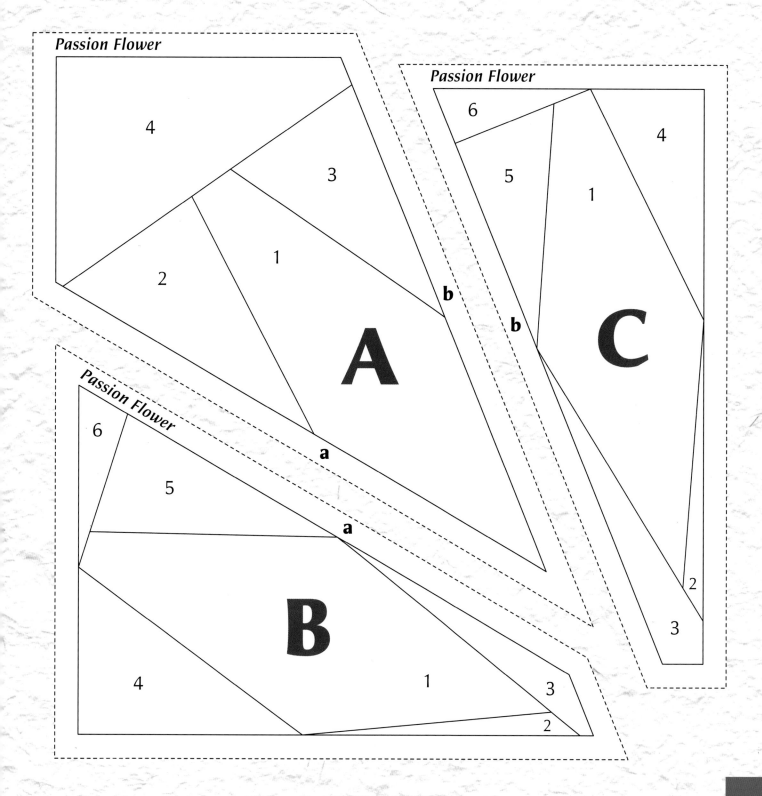

Phlox

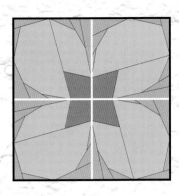

Make 4 of the foundation unit. Join the sections to make the block.

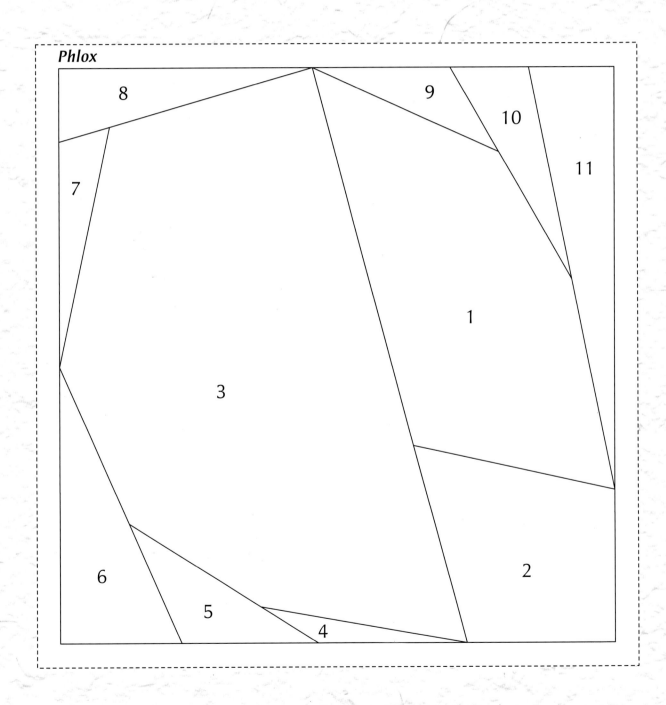

Phlox

8

9

10

7

11

1

3

6

5

4

2

Plumeria

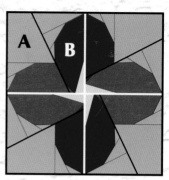

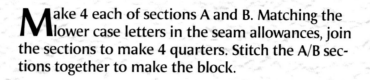

ake 4 each of sections A and B. Matching the lower case letters in the seam allowances, join the sections to make 4 quarters. Stitch the A/B sections together to make the block.

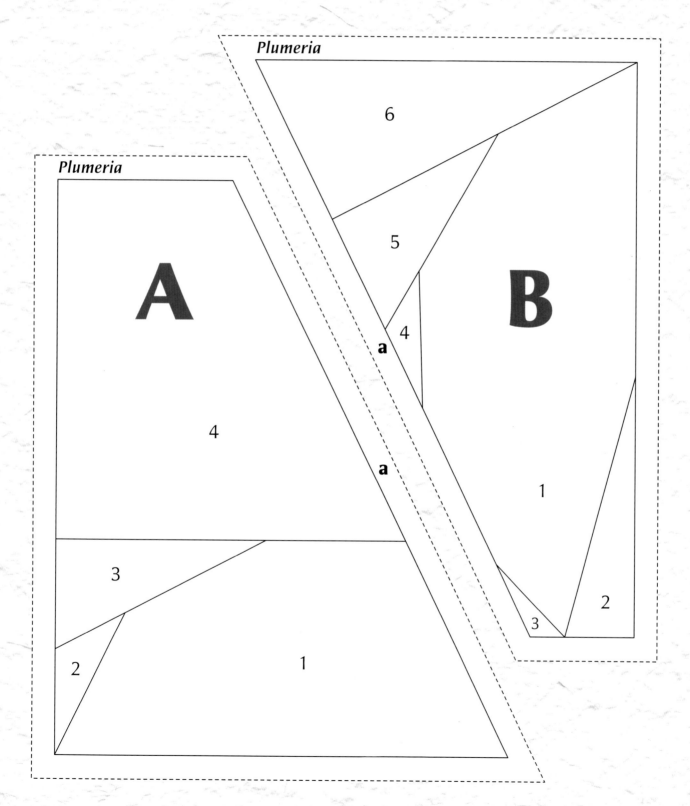

Plumeria

Plumeria

A

B

6

5

4

a

a

4

1

3

2

3

2

1

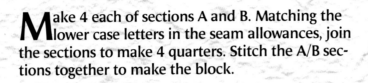

Poinsettia

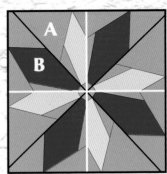

Make 4 each of sections A and B. Matching the lower case letters in the seam allowances, join the sections to make 4 quarters. Stitch the A/B sections together to make the block.

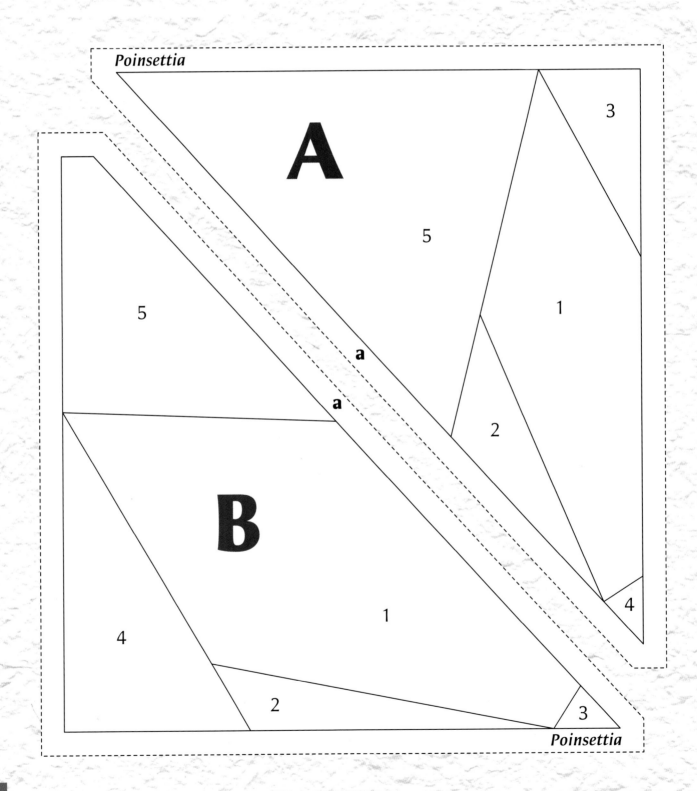

Poinsettia

A

3

5

1

5

a

a

2

B

1

4

4

2

3

Poinsettia

*R*ose

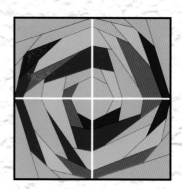

Make 4 of the foundation unit. Join the sections to make the block.

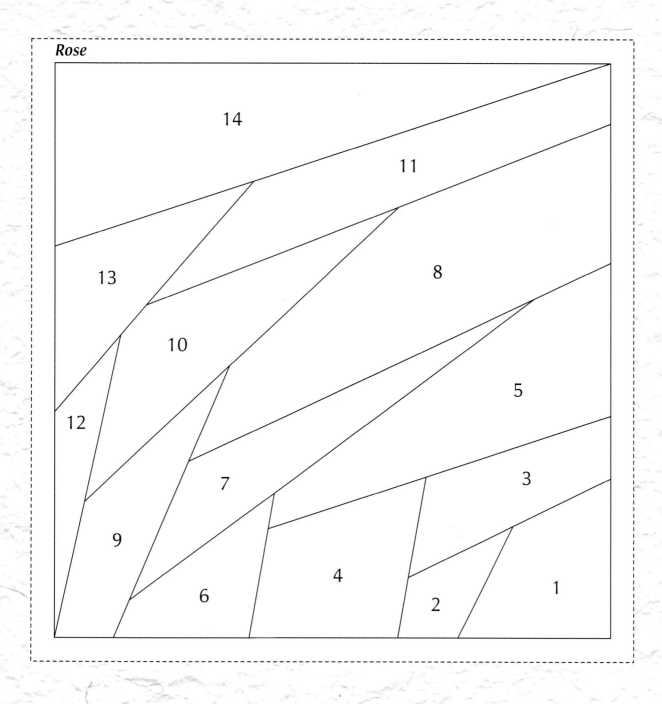

Rose

14

11

13

8

10

12

5

7

3

9

4

6

2

1

Sunflower

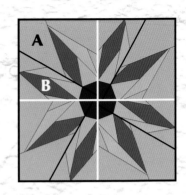

Make 4 each of sections A and B. Matching the lower case letters in the seam allowances, join the sections to make 4 quarters. Stitch the A/B sections together to make the block.

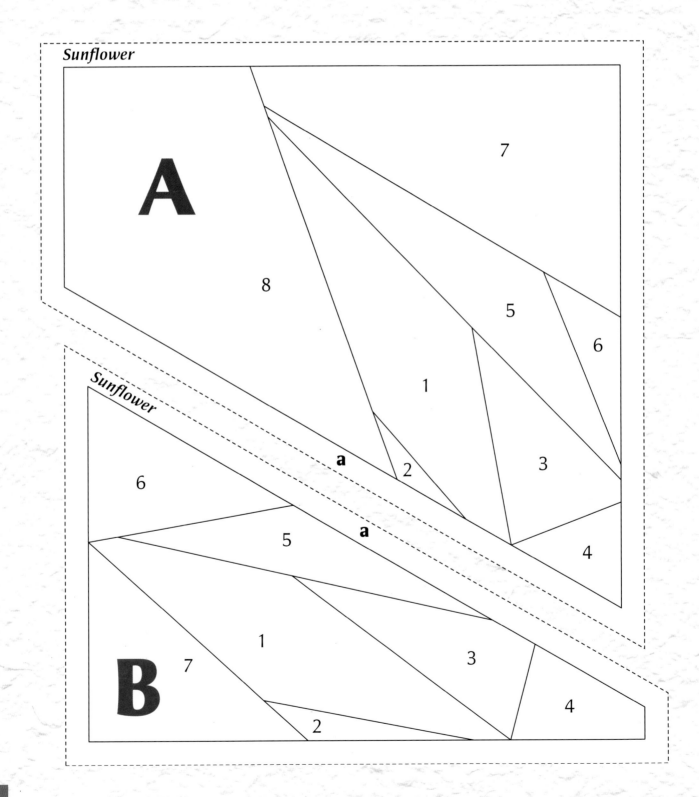

Zinnia

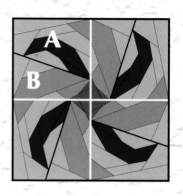

Make 4 each of sections A and B. Matching the lower case letters in the seam allowances, join the sections to make 4 quarters. Stitch the A/B sections together to make the block.

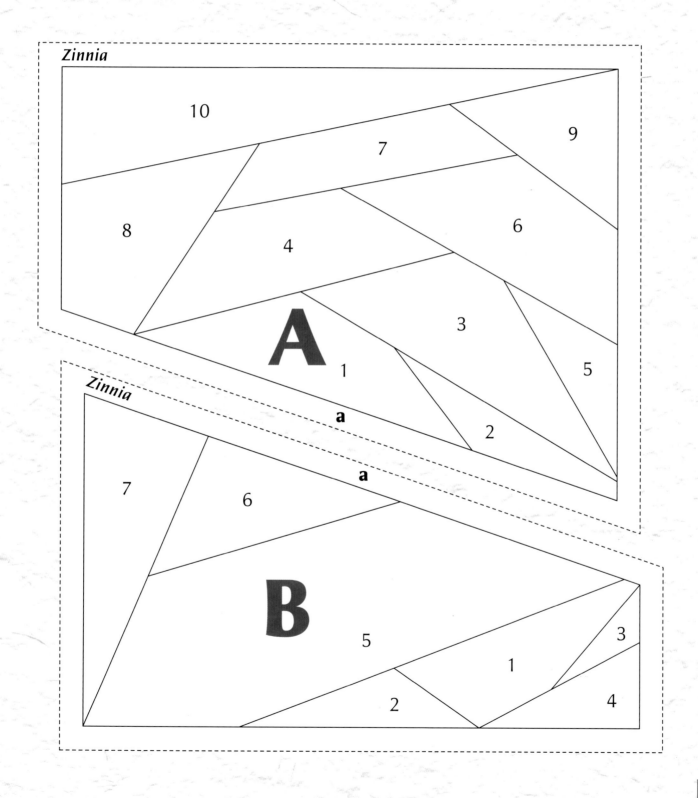

Zinnia

10

9

7

8

6

4

A

3

1

5

a

2

Zinnia

a

7

6

B

5

3

1

2

4

Center Medallion

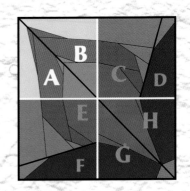

Make 4 each of sections A and B. Matching the lower case letters in the seam allowances, join units A and B to make 4 square A/B units.

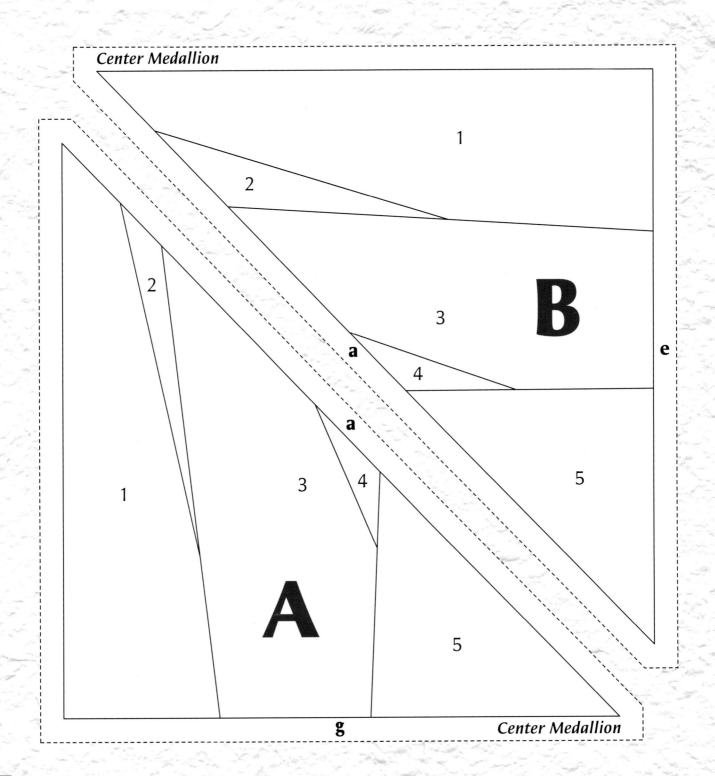

Center Medallion

1

2

2

a

3

B

4

e

a

1

3

4

5

A

5

g   Center Medallion

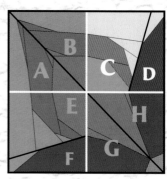

*C*enter Medallion

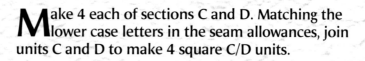

Make 4 each of sections C and D. Matching the lower case letters in the seam allowances, join units C and D to make 4 square C/D units.

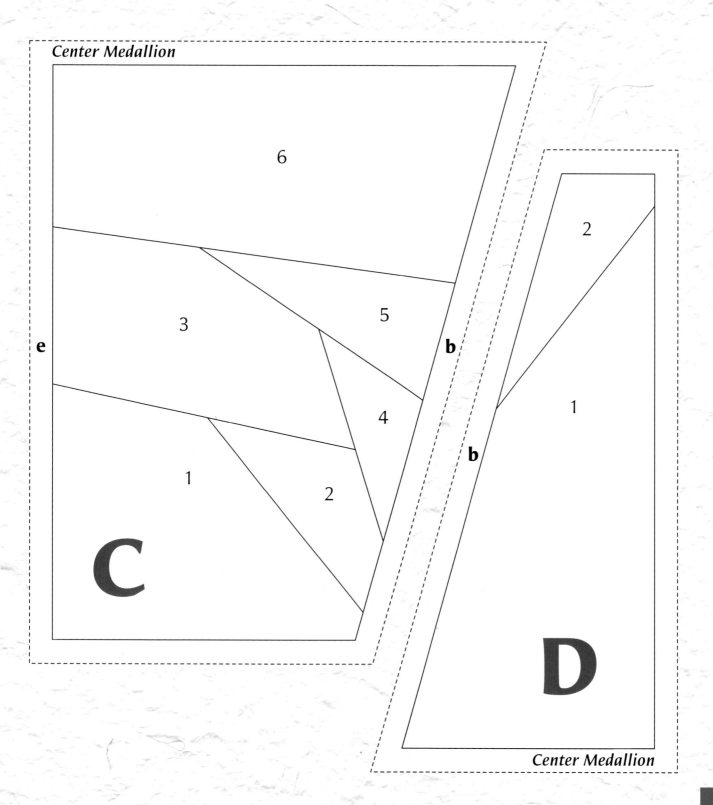

Center Medallion

6

3

5

e

b

b

4

1

2

C

2

1

D

Center Medallion

Center Medallion

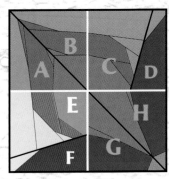

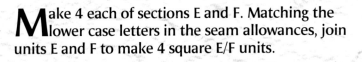

Make 4 each of sections E and F. Matching the lower case letters in the seam allowances, join units E and F to make 4 square E/F units.

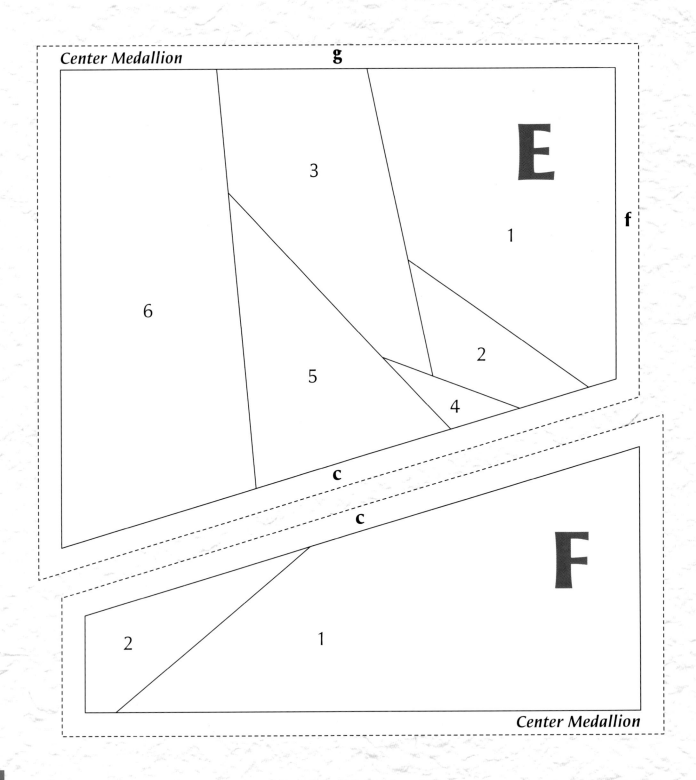

Center Medallion

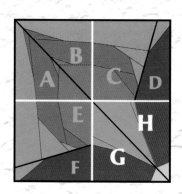

Make 4 each of units G and H. Matching the lower case letters in the seam allowances, join units G and H. Stitch units A/B, C/D, E/F, and G/H into quarters and join them to make the medallion.

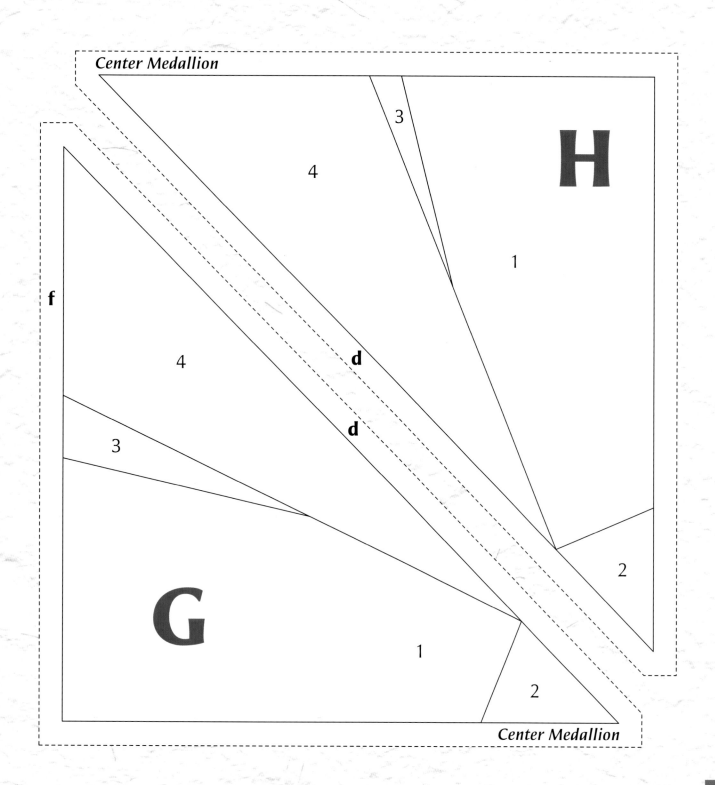

Center Medallion

H

3

4

1

f

4

d

d

3

2

G

1

2

Center Medallion

*L*eaves

Make 40 each of sections A and B. Set the completed units aside until the remaining blocks and sections are completed.

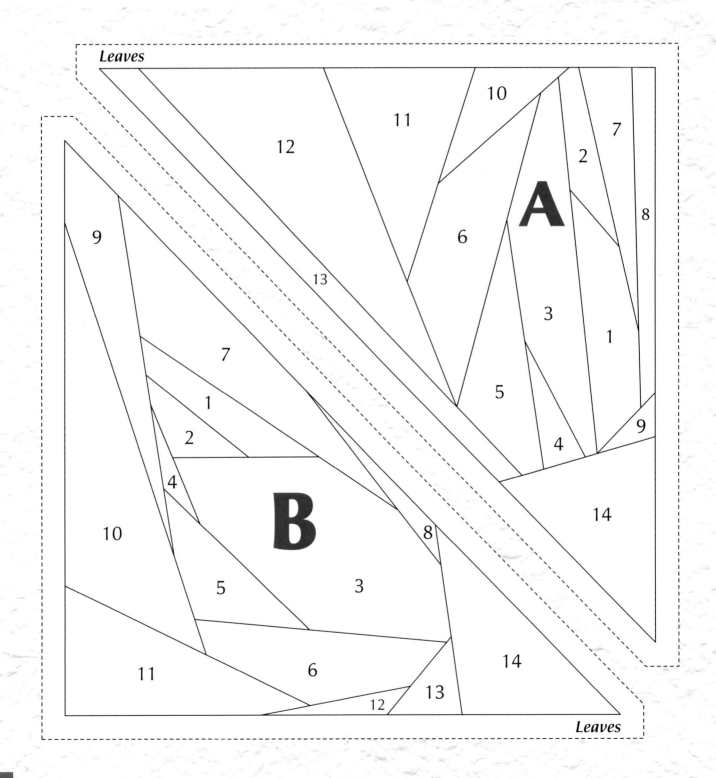

*B*order

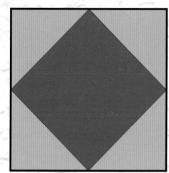

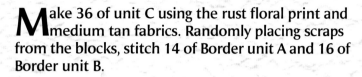

Make 36 of unit C using the rust floral print and medium tan fabrics. Randomly placing scraps from the blocks, stitch 14 of Border unit A and 16 of Border unit B.

Border

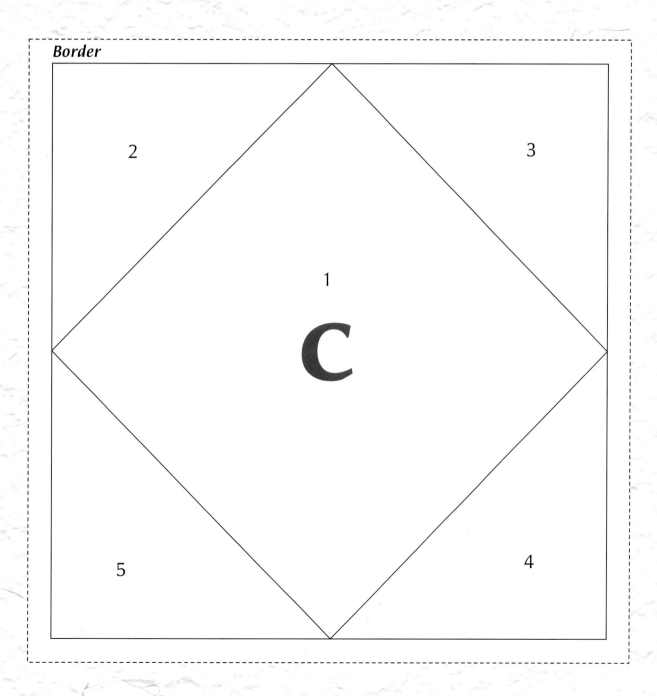

2

3

1

C

5

4

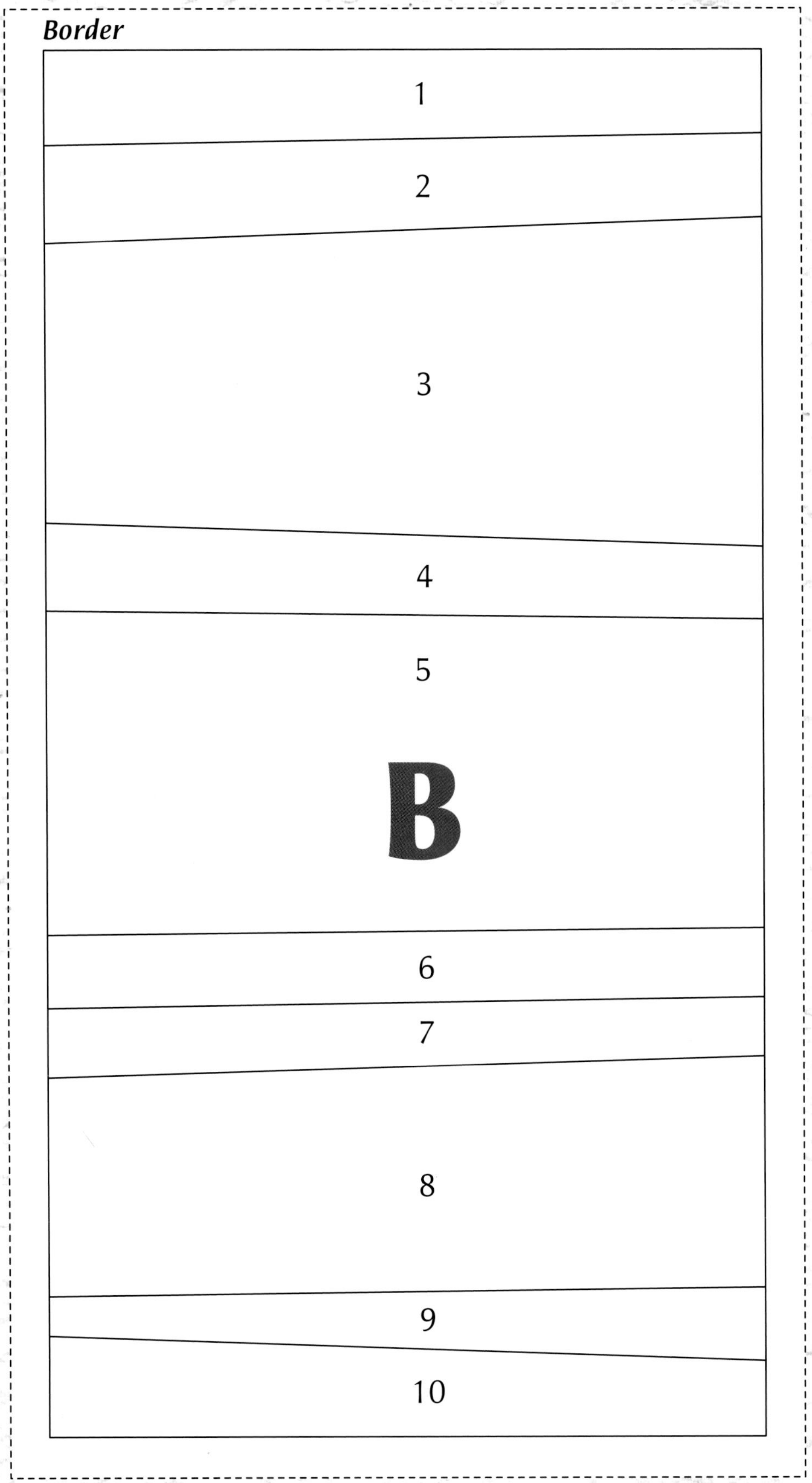

Border

1

2

3

4

5

B

6

7

8

9

10

Border

A

1

2

3

4

5

6

7

8

9

10

*F*resh Cut Flowers
woodcut quilt

*M*aterials

Quilt Size: 84" x 102"

4¾ yds. light tan (background for leaves and
  center medallion)
7½ yds. medium tan (background for flower
  blocks and Border section C)

1 yd. orange (border section C)
1 yd. medium green (leaves)
1¼ yds. dark green (leaves)
9½ yds. black (woodcut)

Fabric	Block(s)	Fabric	Block(s)
¼ yd. light mauve	Impatiens, Plumeria,	1 yd. medium green	Aster, Clematis, Cosmos, Dahlia, Hosta, Magnolia, Lily of the Valley
½ yd. medium mauve	Cactus Flower, Chrysanthemum, Cosmos, Poinsettia	¾ yd. dark green	Aster, Campanula, Chrysanthemum, Geranium, Hosta, Magnolia
½ yd. dark mauve	Chrysanthemum, Cosmos, Impatiens, Poinsettia	½ yd. light blue	Campanula, Hydrangea
¼ yd. light magenta	Dahlia	¾ yd. medium blue	Aster, Clematis, Phlox, Japanese Iris, Zinnia
½ yd. medium magenta	Cactus Flower, California Poppy, Dahlia, Zinnia	1 yd. dark blue	Japanese Iris, Sunflower, Center Medallion
¼ yd. dark magenta	California Poppy	1¼ yds. light purple	Clematis, Crocus, Japanese Iris, Phlox, Passion Flower, Center Medallion
½ yd. medium red	California Poppy, Geranium		
¼ yd. dark red	California Poppy, Geranium	1¼ yds. medium purple	Anemone, Passion Flower, Plumeria, Phlox, California Poppy, Center Medallion
½ yd. orange	Cactus Flower, Daffodil, Passion Flower		
½ yd. light yellow	Black Eyed Susan, Magnolia, Rose	1½ yds. dark purple	Anemone, Aster, Chrysanthemum , Crocus, Clematis, Japanese Iris, Passion Flower, Plumeria, Zinnia
¾ yd. medium yellow	Black Eyed Susan, Crocus, Daffodil, Marigold, Rose		
½ yd. dark yellow	Black Eyed Susan, Cactus Flower, Rose		
½ yd. white	Dogwood Blossom, Lily of the Valley, Magnolia	½ yd. light brown	Anemone, Hydrangea
		1 yd. medium brown	Black Eyed Susan, Daffodil, Marigold, Sunflower, Center Medallion
¾ yd. light green	Aster, Campanula, Hosta, Poinsettia, Lily of the Valley	½ yd. dark brown	Dogwood Blossom, Hosta, Sunflower

Border sections A and B are made using randomly placed scraps from the fabrics used in the blocks

Making the Quilt Top

1 Make one each of the following blocks: Anemone, Aster, Black Eyed Susan, Cactus Flower, California Poppy, Campanula, Chrysanthemum, Clematis, Cosmos, Crocus, Daffodil, Dahlia, Dogwood Blossom, Geranium, Hosta, Hydrangea, Impatiens, Japanese Iris, Lily of the Valley, Magnolia, Marigold, Passion Flower, Phlox, Plumeria, Poinsettia, Rose, Sunflower, Zinnia, and the Center Medallion.

2 Using the medium green, dark green, and light tan fabrics, make 40 each of the Leaf sections A and B. Do not assemble these subunits into blocks yet, they need to be joined in a specific way to construct the quilt.

3 Using the orange and medium tan fabrics, make 36 of Border section C.

4 Using the scraps left over from piecing the blocks, make 14 of Border section A and 16 of Border unit B. Place the colors within each section randomly, using black for the light grey shaded areas (woodcut) of the design.

5 Flip all of the completed blocks and units to the printed side (fabric side down) and arrange them as shown in the **Quilt Assembly Diagram** (see page 59).

6 Starting at the center of the quilt, construct the 2 short diagonal rows that attach to the sides of the medallion. Referring to the **Quilt Assembly Diagram**, join the sections and attach them to the medallion.

7 Stitch the remaining six diagonal rows that comprise the inner portion of the quilt top and join them to the center medallion.

8 Make 2 inner side border strips, each containing 8 of Border section B. Add these strips to the left and right sides of the quilt top. Make the remaining 2 inner border strips using 7 Border A sections per strip; stitch these strips to the top and bottom edges.

9 Using the remaining blocks and border sections, make the side border strips. Stitch these strips to the left and right sides of the quilt top. Join the blocks and sections to make the upper and lower border strips and add these strips to the top and bottom edges.

Finishing the Quilt

1 Remove the paper from the back of the quilt top. If you have trouble removing the paper from tight areas, use a pair of tweezers to help reach into tough spots.

2 Layer the quilt top with batting and backing. Baste the layers together.

3 Machine quilt "in the ditch" around each of the flowers and leaves to hold the layers in place. Stipple the light tan background areas in the center of the quilt surrounding the leaves and medallion. Free-motion quilt a leaf design in the inner border and add softly curving lines in the petals of the flowers and center medallion. Quilt floral designs in the center of the outer border blocks

4 Embellish the flowers with beads, decorative quilting with metallic thread, or embroidery to add an extra dimension to your quilt.

Quilt Assembly Diagram
(view from marked side of foundations)

Anemone

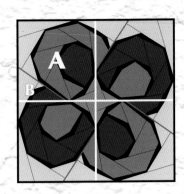

Make 4 each of sections A and B. Matching the lower case letters in the seam allowances, join the sections to make 4 quarters. Stitch the A/B sections together to make the block.

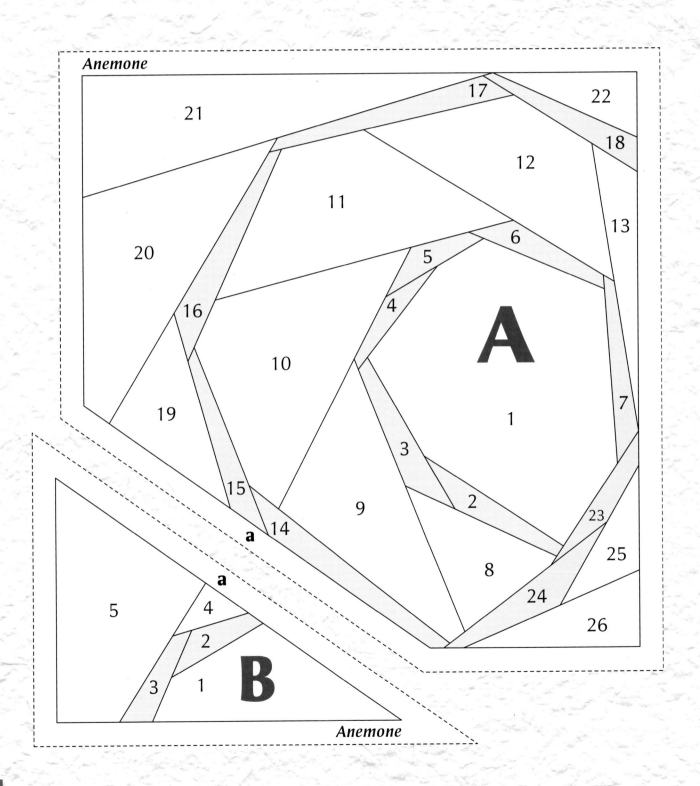

Anemone

21

17   22

18

12

11

20   13

6

5

16   4

A

10

19   7

1

3

15

2

14   9

a

8   23

a   25

5   4

2   24

3   1   B   26

Anemone

*A*ster

Make 4 each of sections A and B. Matching the lower case letters in the seam allowances, join the sections to make 4 quarters. Stitch the A/B sections together to make the block.

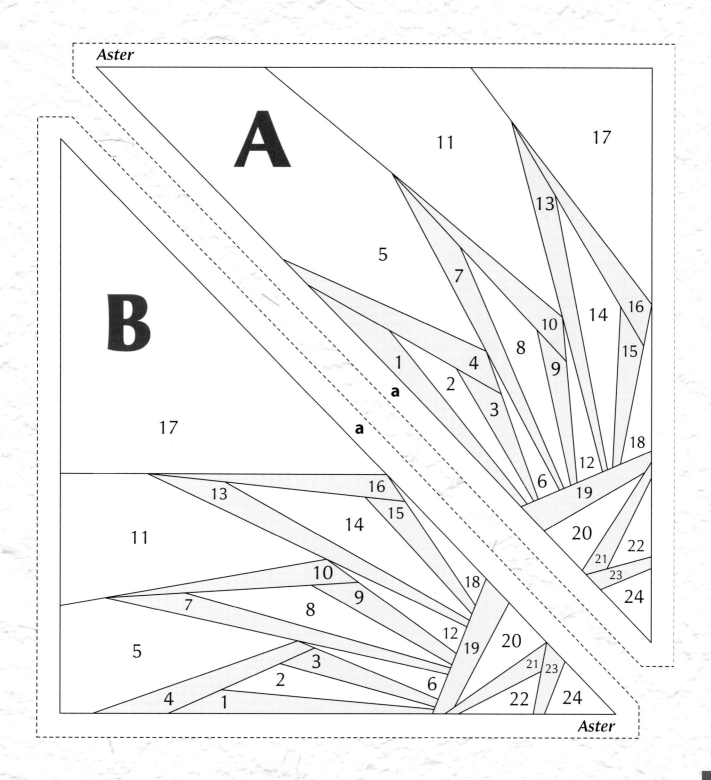

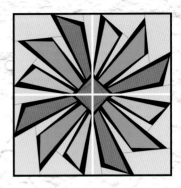

*B*lack Eyed Susan

*M*ake 4 of the foundation unit. Join the sections to make the block.

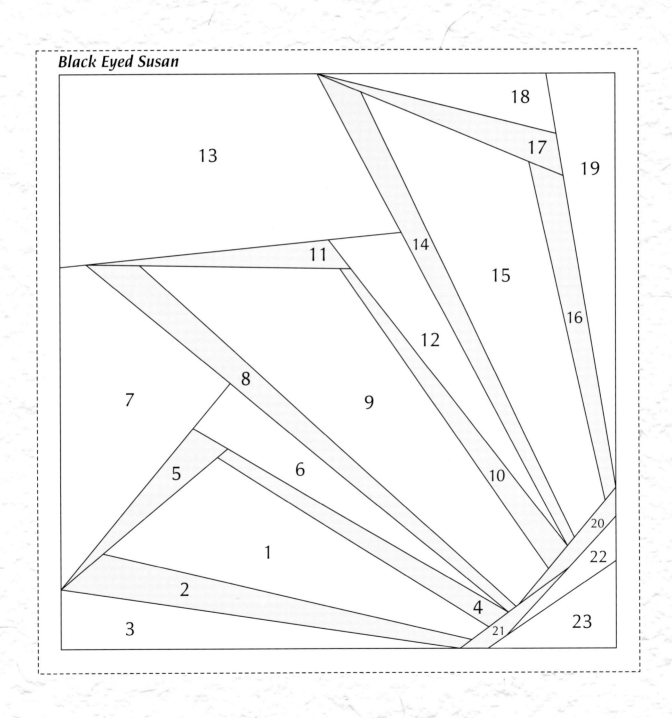

Black Eyed Susan

13

18

17

19

11

14

15

16

12

8

7

9

5

6

10

1

2

4

20

22

3

21

23

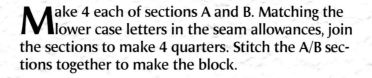

Cactus Flower

Make 4 each of sections A and B. Matching the lower case letters in the seam allowances, join the sections to make 4 quarters. Stitch the A/B sections together to make the block.

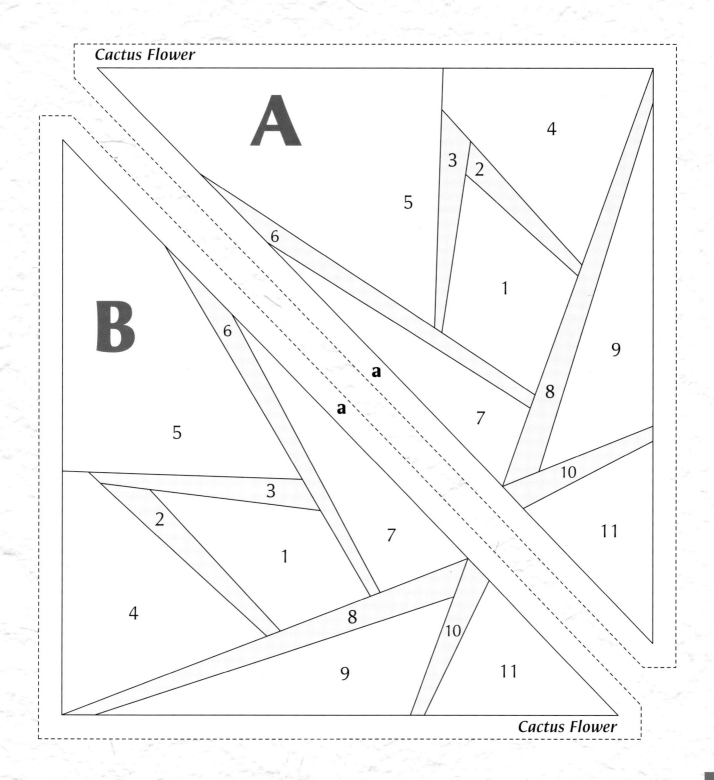

Cactus Flower

A

4

3 2

5

6

1

6

9

B

a

8

5

a

7

3

10

2

7

1

11

4

8

10

9

11

Cactus Flower

California Poppy

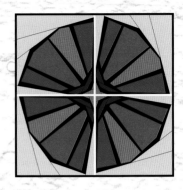

Make 4 of the foundation unit. Join the sections to make the block.

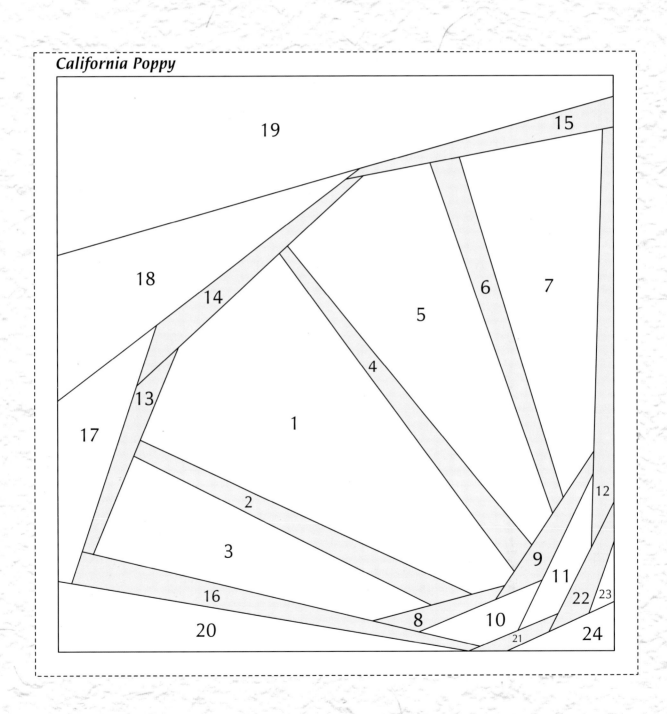

California Poppy

19
15
18
14
6 7
5
4
13
17
1
12
2
3
9
11
16
8 10 22 23
20 21 24

Campanula

M̲ake 4 each of sections A and B. Matching the lower case letters in the seam allowances, join the sections to make 4 quarters. Stitch the A/B sections together to make the block.

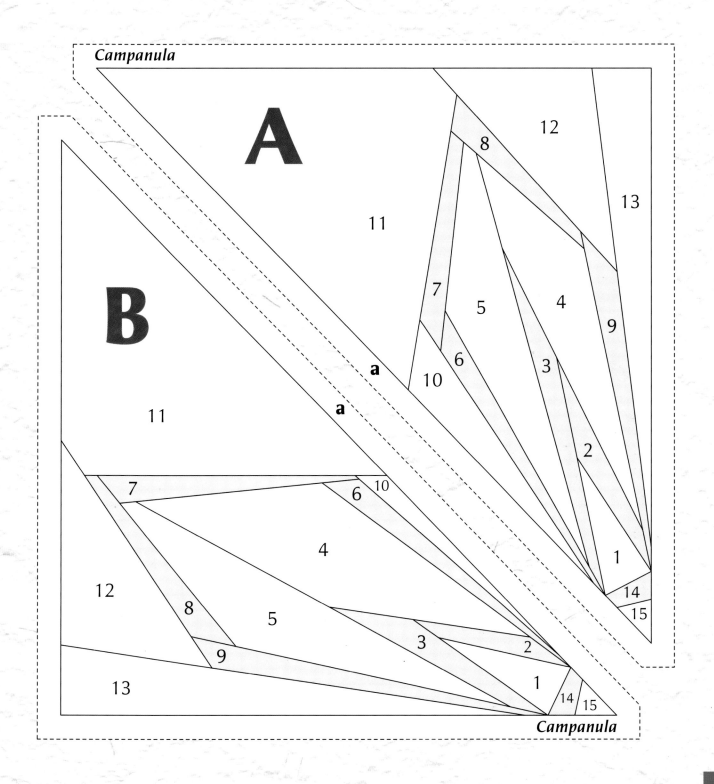

Chrysanthemum

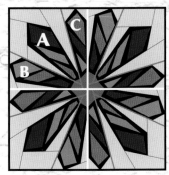

Make 4 each of sections A—C. Matching the lower case letters in the seam allowances, join the sections to make 4 quarters. Stitch the A/B/C sections together to make the block.

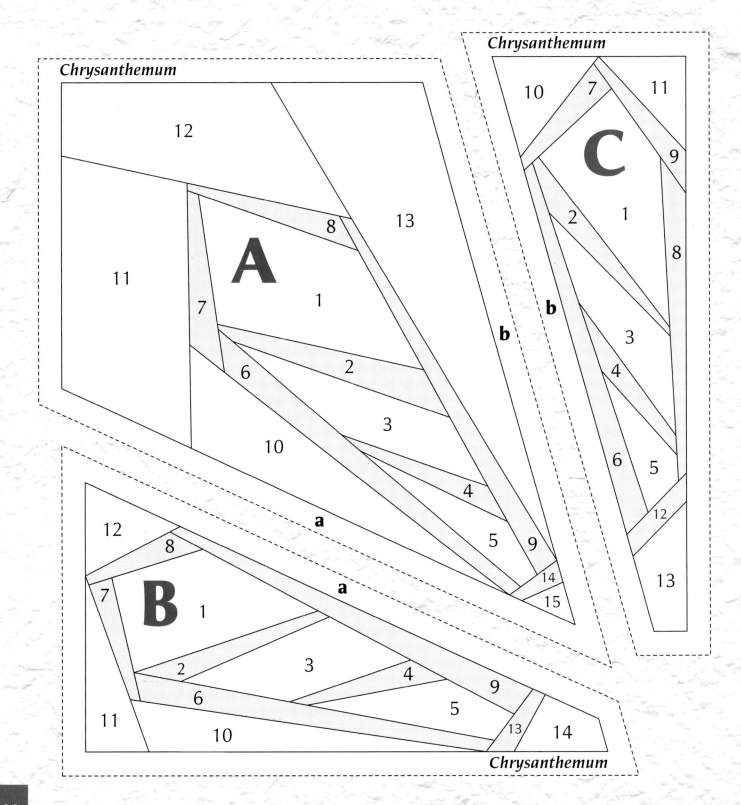

Chrysanthemum

12

11

8

A

13

7

1

6

2

10

3

4

a

5

9

a

14

15

Chrysanthemum

10   7   11

C

9

2   1

b

8

b

3

4

6   5

12

13

Chrysanthemum

12

8

7

B

1

2   3   4

6   9

11

5

10   13   14

Chrysanthemum

Clematis

Make 4 each of sections A—D. Matching the lower case letters in the seam allowances, join the sections to make 4 quarters. Stitch the A/B/C/D sections together to make the block.

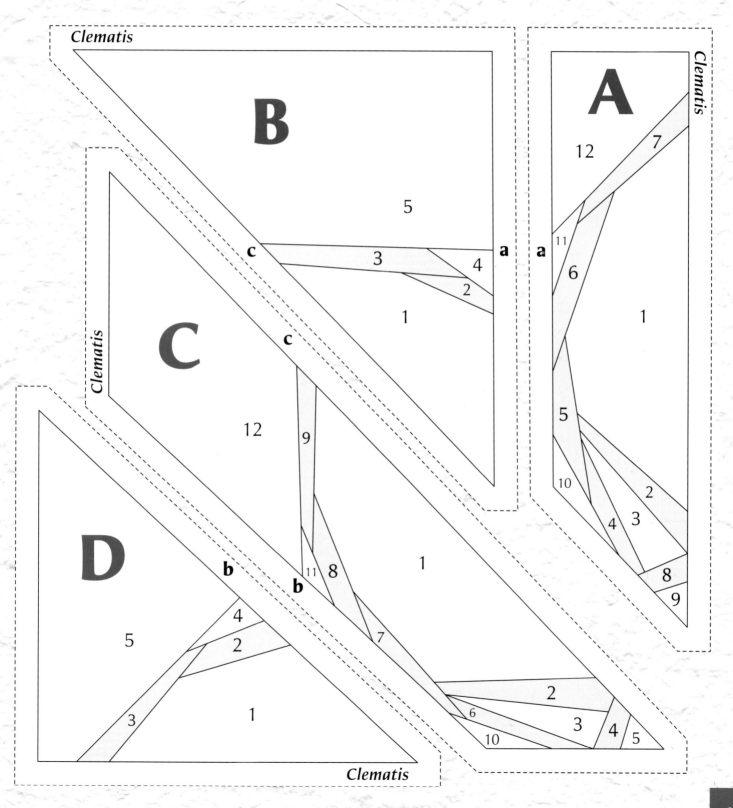

Clematis

B

5

c

3

4

a

2

1

A

Clematis

12

7

11

6

1

5

10

2

4

3

8

9

a

a

Clematis

C

c

12

9

11 8

1

D

b

b

4

2

7

5

2

1

3

6

3

4 5

10

Clematis

Cosmos

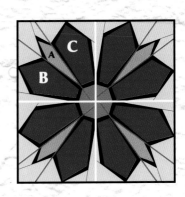

Make 4 each of sections A—C. Matching the lower case letters in the seam allowances, join the sections to make 4 quarters. Stitch the A/B/C sections together to make the block.

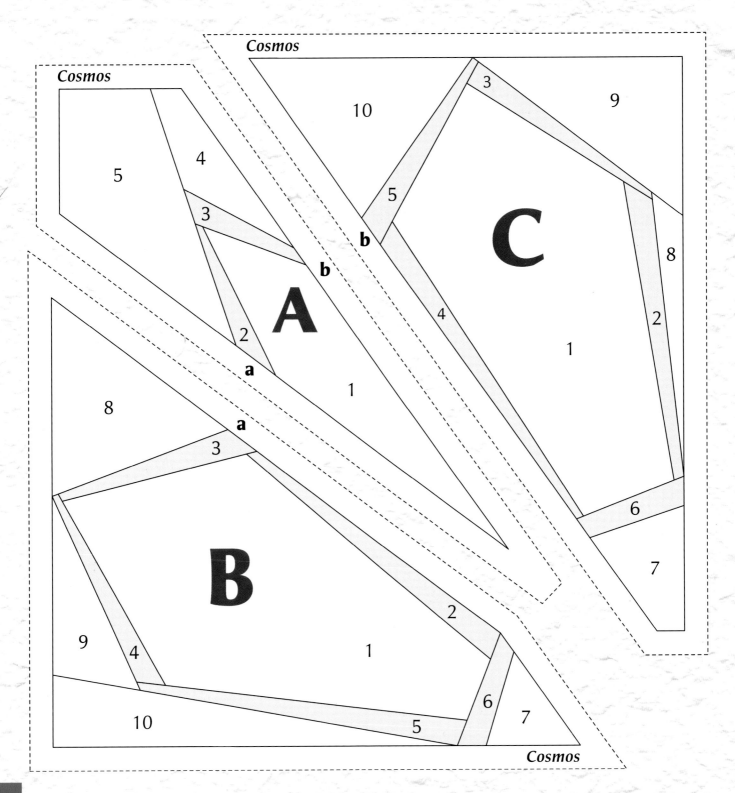

Cosmos

Cosmos

Cosmos

5

4

3

2

a

A

1

10

3

9

5

b

b

4

C

8

2

1

6

7

8

3

a

B

9

4

1

2

10

5

6

7

Crocus

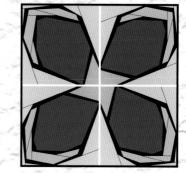

Make 4 of the foundation unit. Join the sections to make the block.

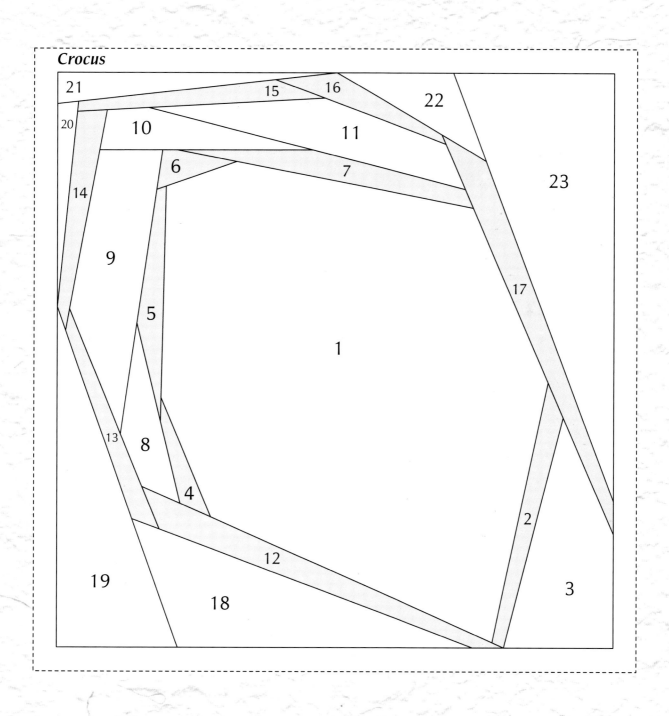

Crocus

21 20 10 15 16 22

14 6 7 11 23

9

5 17

1

13 8

4 2

12 3

19 18

*D*affodil

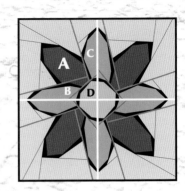

Make 4 each of sections A—D. Matching the lower case letters in the seam allowances, join the sections to make 4 quarters. Stitch the A/B/C/D sections together to make the block.

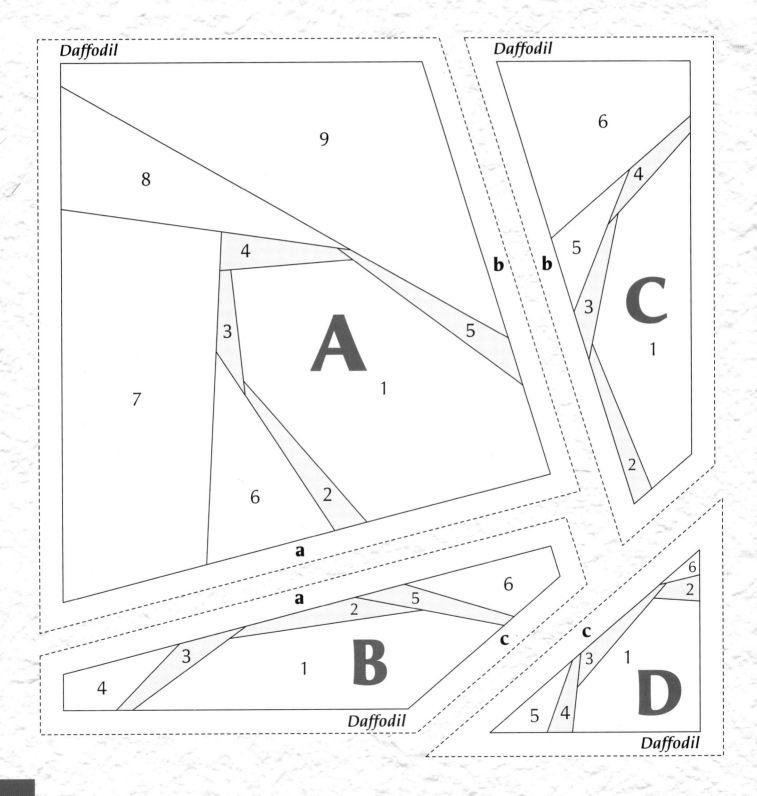

Dahlia

Make 4 each of sections A and B. Matching the lower case letters in the seam allowances, join the sections to make 4 quarters. Stitch the A/B sections together to make the block.

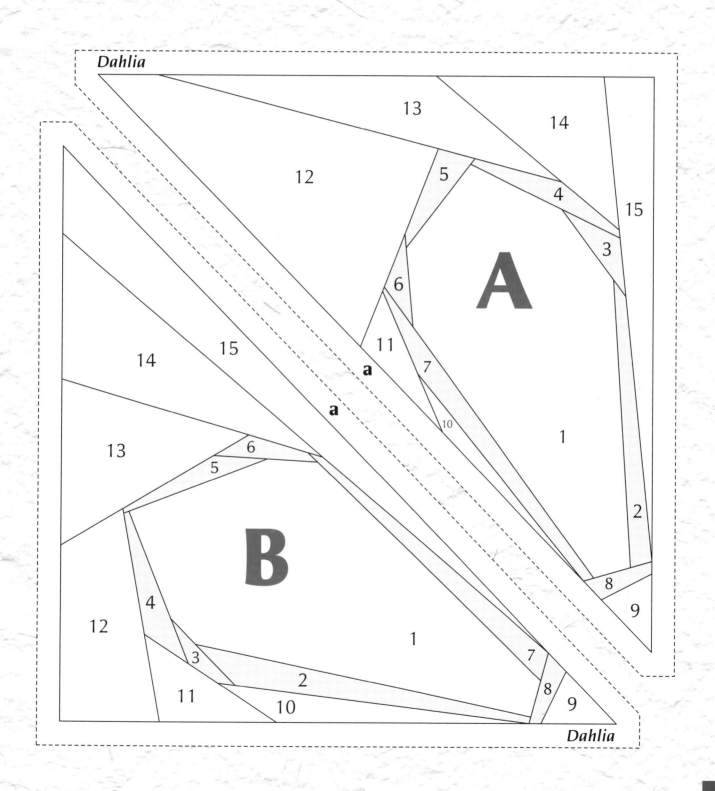

Dahlia

13
14
12
5
4
15
3
6
A
11
7
a
a
10
1
2
15
14
13
6
5
B
4
12
3
1
7
2
8
11
10
9
8
9

Dahlia

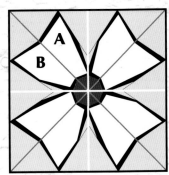

Dogwood Blossom

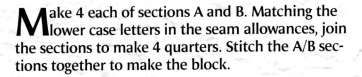

Make 4 each of sections A and B. Matching the lower case letters in the seam allowances, join the sections to make 4 quarters. Stitch the A/B sections together to make the block.

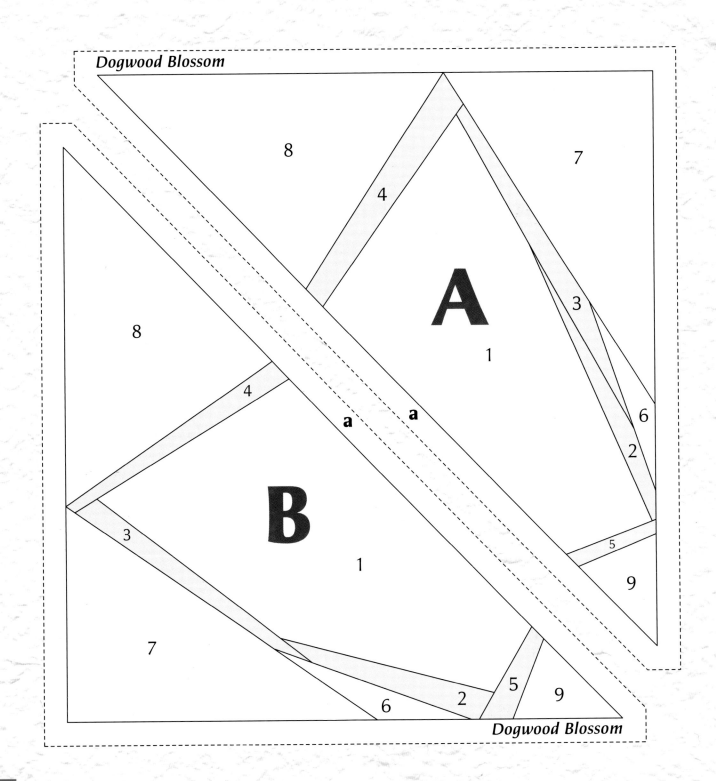

Dogwood Blossom

8

7

4

8

A

1

3

4

a   **a**

6

2

B

3

1

5

9

7

5

9

6   2

Dogwood Blossom

Geranium

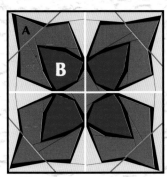

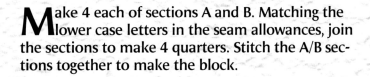

Make 4 each of sections A and B. Matching the lower case letters in the seam allowances, join the sections to make 4 quarters. Stitch the A/B sections together to make the block.

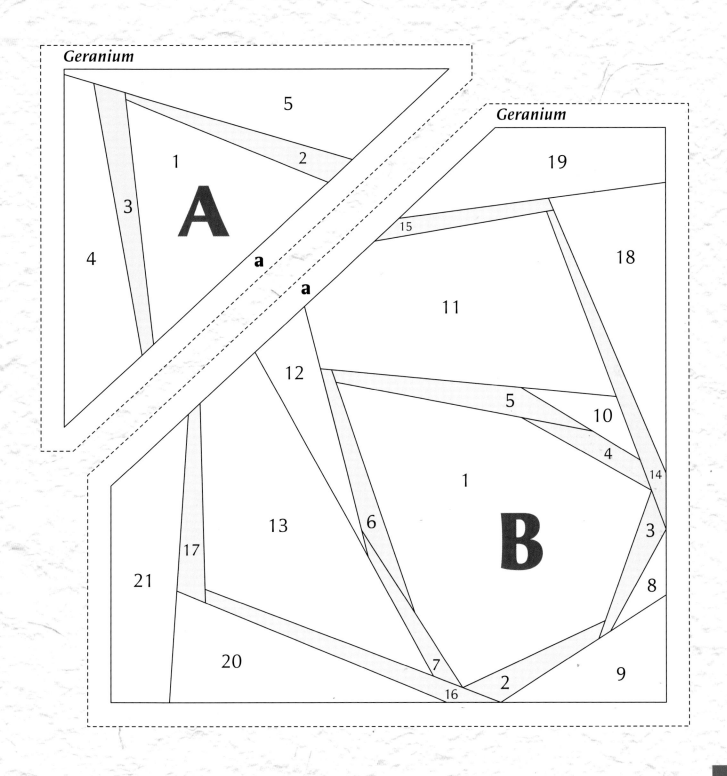

Geranium

5

1   2

A

3

4

a

a

Geranium

19

15

18

11

5

10

12

4

14

1

3

B

13

6

8

17

21

20

7

2   9

16

Hosta

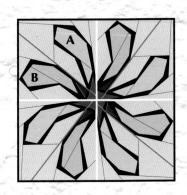

Make 4 each of sections A and B. Matching the lower case letters in the seam allowances, join the sections to make 4 quarters. Stitch the A/B sections together to make the block.

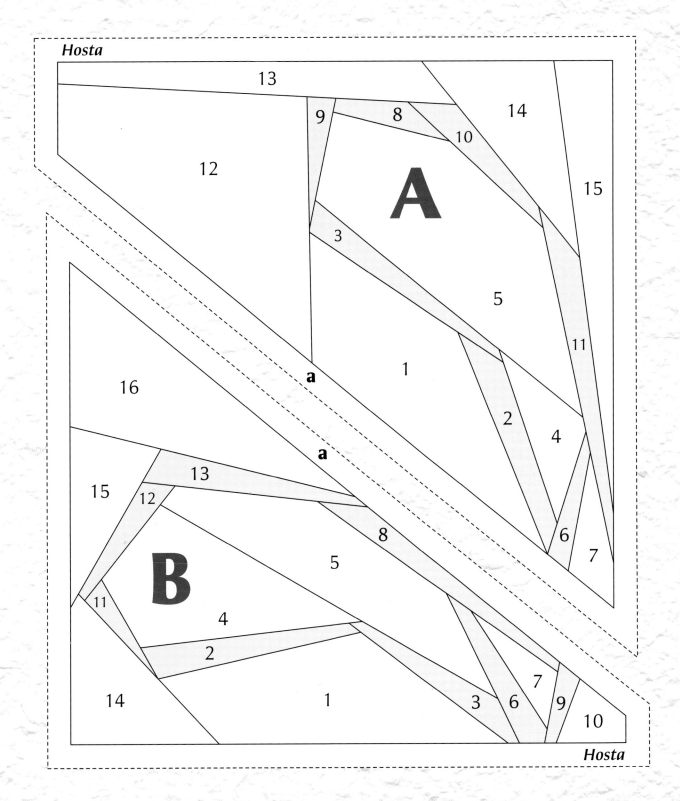

Hosta

13

9   8   14

10

12

A

15

3

5

11

a

1

2   4

16

a

13

15   12

8   6   7

5

B

4

11

2

7

14   1   3   6   9

10

Hosta

Hydrangea

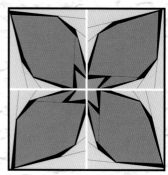

Make 4 of the foundation unit. Join the sections to make the block.

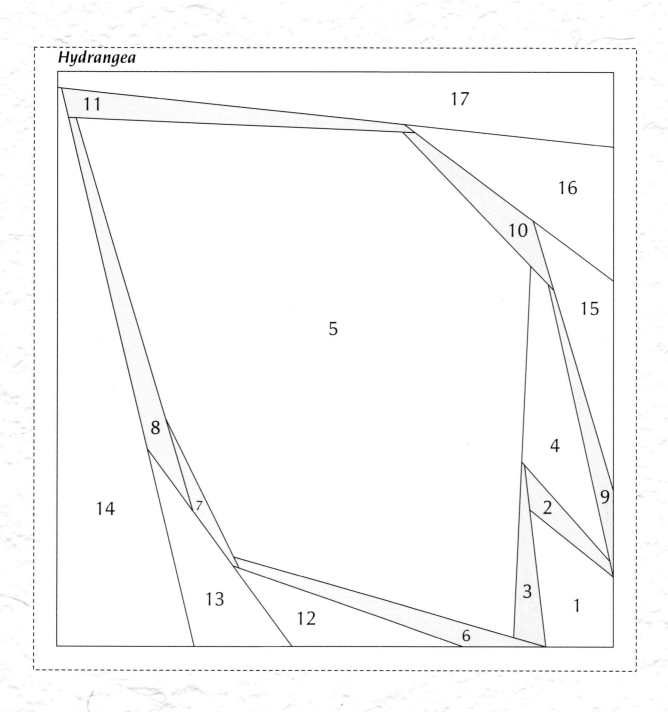

Hydrangea

11   17

16

10

15

5

4

8

9

7

2

14

3

1

13

12

6

Impatiens

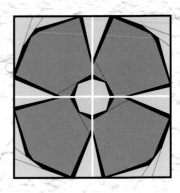

Make 4 of the foundation unit. Join the sections to make the block.

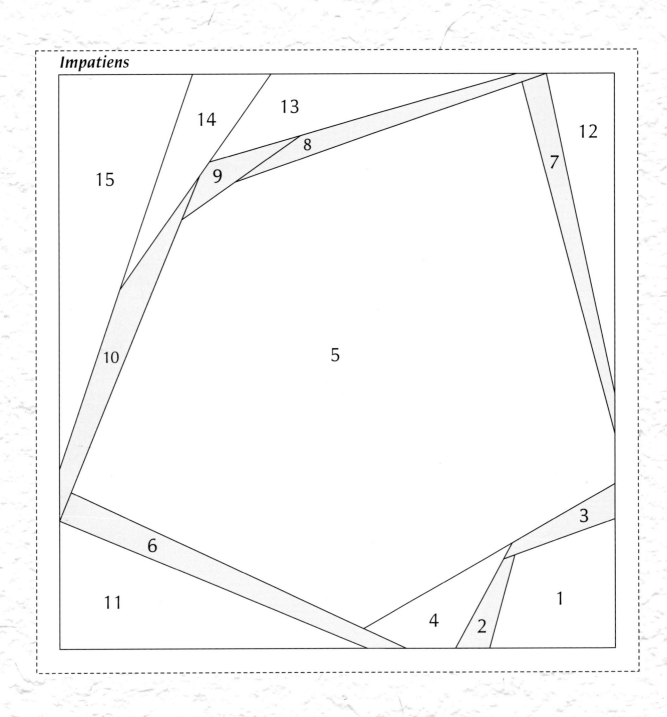

Impatiens

14

13

15

8

9

12

7

10

5

3

6

11

4

2

1

Japanese Iris

Make 4 each of sections A—C. Matching the lower case letters in the seam allowances, join the sections to make 4 quarters. Stitch the A/B/C sections together to make the block.

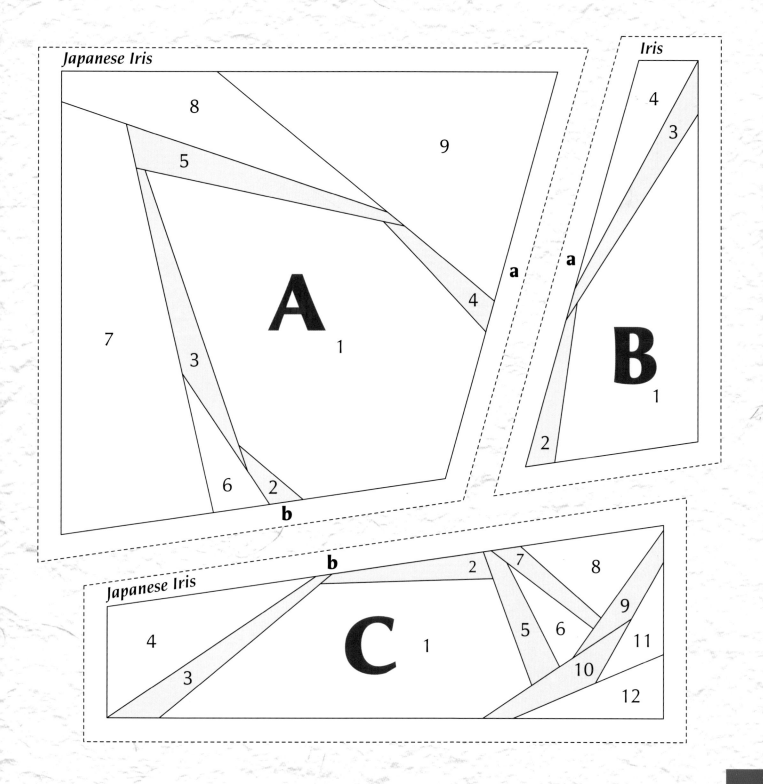

Lily of the Valley

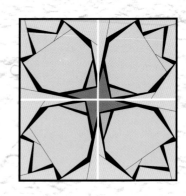

Make 4 of the foundation unit. Join the sections to make the block.

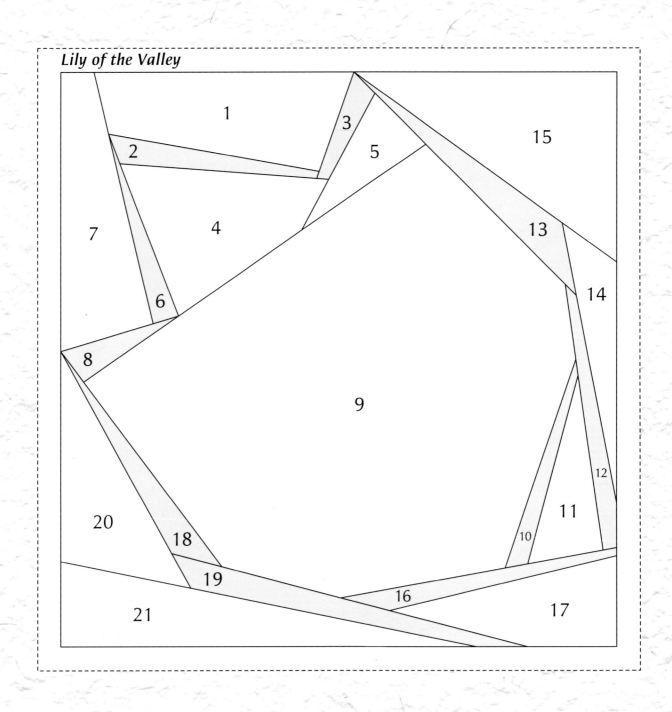

Lily of the Valley

1

2

3

5

15

7

4

13

14

6

12

8

9

11

10

20

18

19

16

17

21

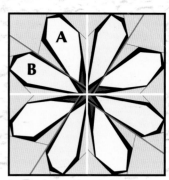

*M*agnolia

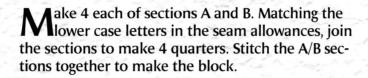

*M*ake 4 each of sections A and B. Matching the lower case letters in the seam allowances, join the sections to make 4 quarters. Stitch the A/B sections together to make the block.

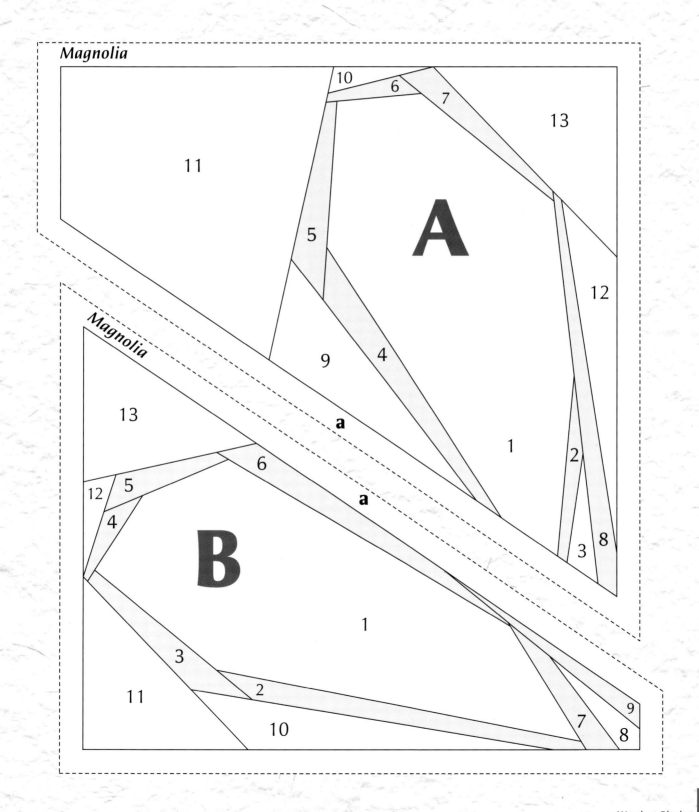

Magnolia

10 6 7

13

11

5

A

12

9 4

a

1

2

a

3 8

Magnolia

13

6

5

12

4

B

1

3

2

11

10

7 9

8

Marigold

Make 4 of the foundation unit. Join the sections to make the block.

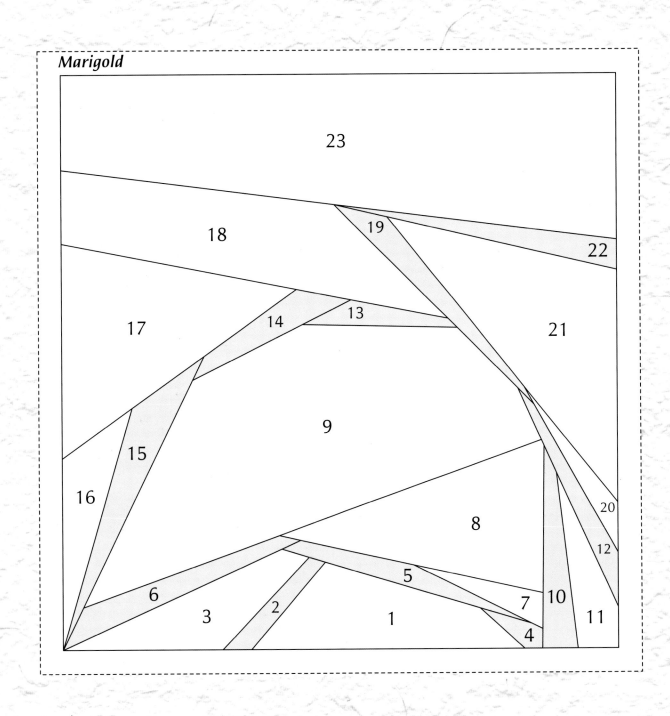

Marigold

23

18

19

22

17

14

13

21

9

15

16

8

20

12

5

6

7

10

3

2

1

11

4

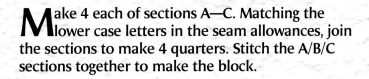

Passion Flower

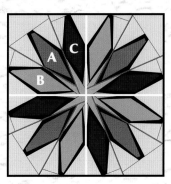

Make 4 each of sections A—C. Matching the lower case letters in the seam allowances, join the sections to make 4 quarters. Stitch the A/B/C sections together to make the block.

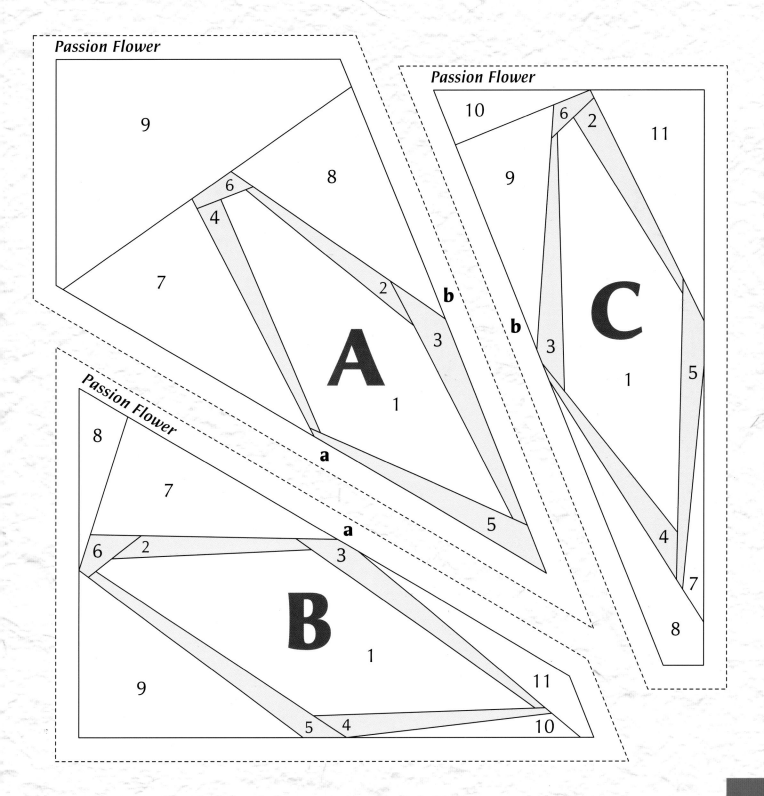

Passion Flower

9

8

6

4

7

2

3

A

1

b

Passion Flower

10

6

2

9

11

b

b

3

C

1

5

4

7

8

a

Passion Flower

8

7

6

2

3

a

B

1

9

5

4

11

10

Phlox

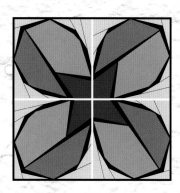

Make 4 of the foundation unit. Join the sections to make the block.

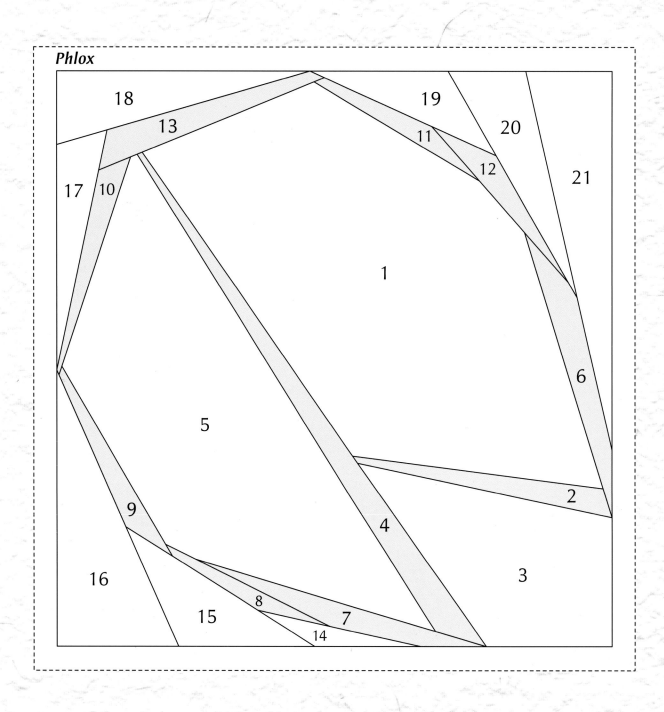

Phlox

18

13

19

20

11

12

21

17

10

1

6

5

9

2

4

16

3

8

15

7

14

*P*lumeria

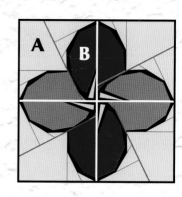

Make 4 each of sections A and B. Matching the lower case letters in the seam allowances, join the sections to make 4 quarters. Stitch the A/B sections together to make the block.

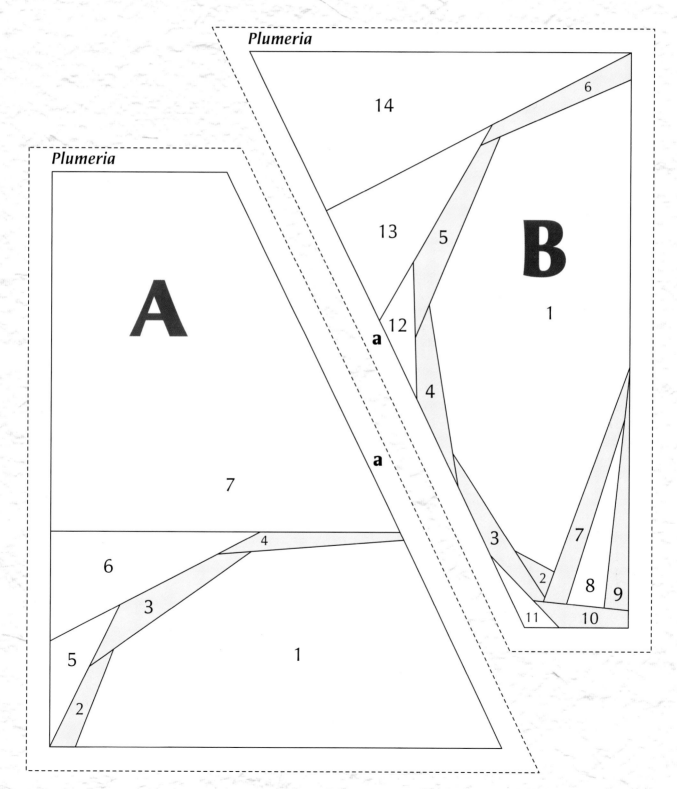

Plumeria

14

6

13

5

B

1

12

a

4

a

A

7

3

7

4

6

2

8 9

3

11 10

5

1

2

Poinsettia

Make 4 each of sections A and B. Matching the lower case letters in the seam allowances, join the sections to make 4 quarters. Stitch the A/B sections together to make the block.

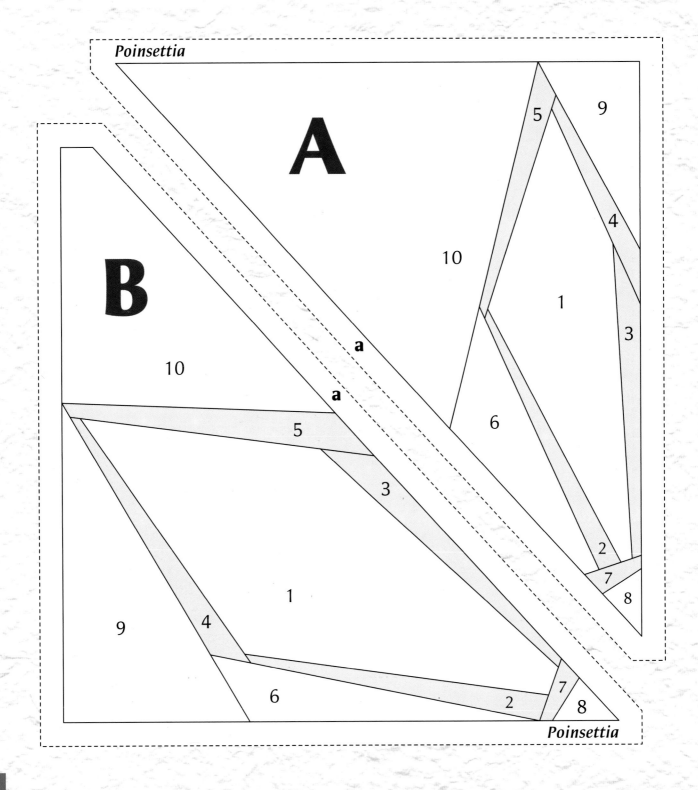

Poinsettia

A

B

5

9

10

4

1

3

a

a

5

6

3

10

2

7

8

1

9

4

6

7

2

8

Poinsettia

Rose

Make 4 of the foundation unit. Join the sections to make the block.

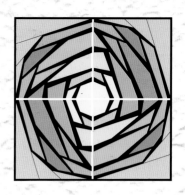

Rose

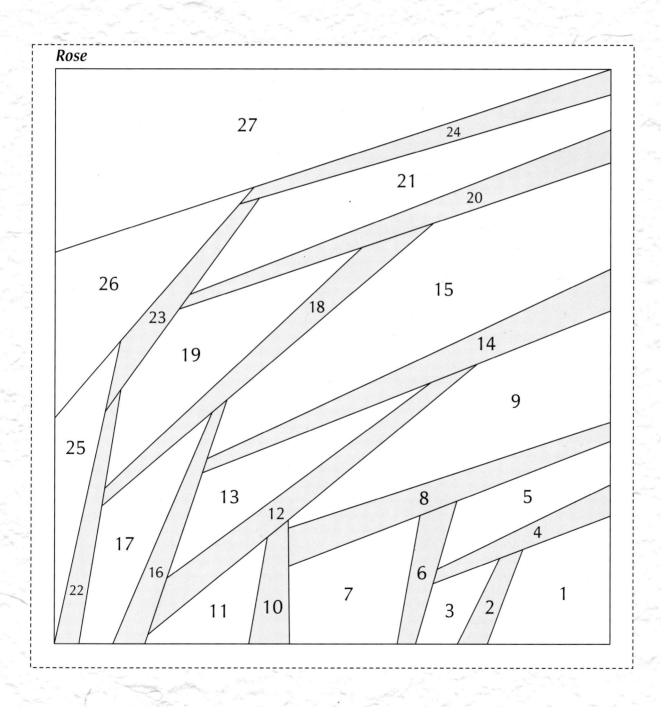

Sunflower

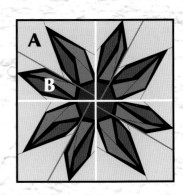

Make 4 each of sections A and B. Matching the lower case letters in the seam allowances, join the sections to make 4 quarters. Stitch the A/B sections together to make the block.

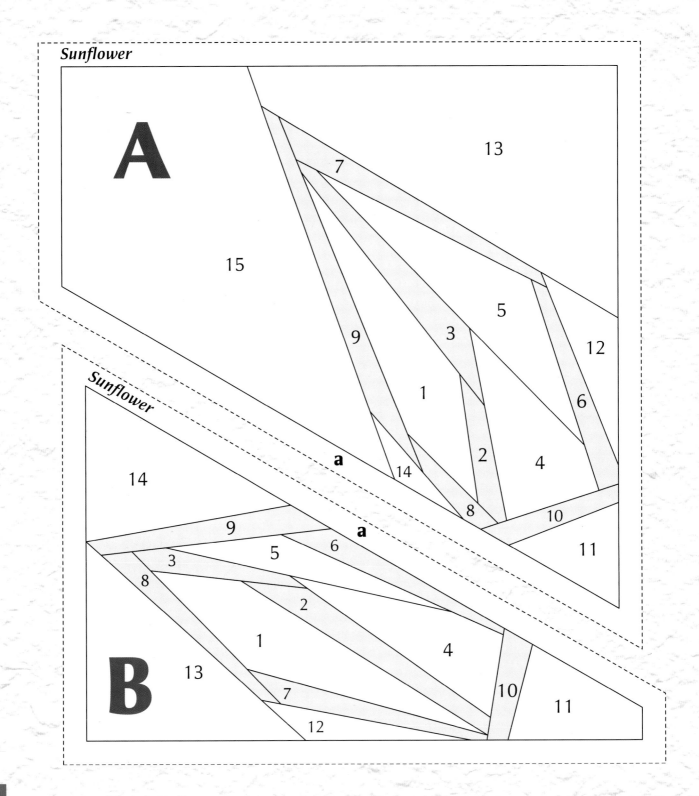

Zinnia

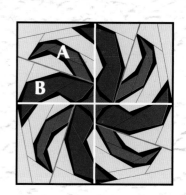

Make 4 each of sections A and B. Matching the lower case letters in the seam allowances, join the sections to make 4 quarters. Stitch the A/B sections together to make the block.

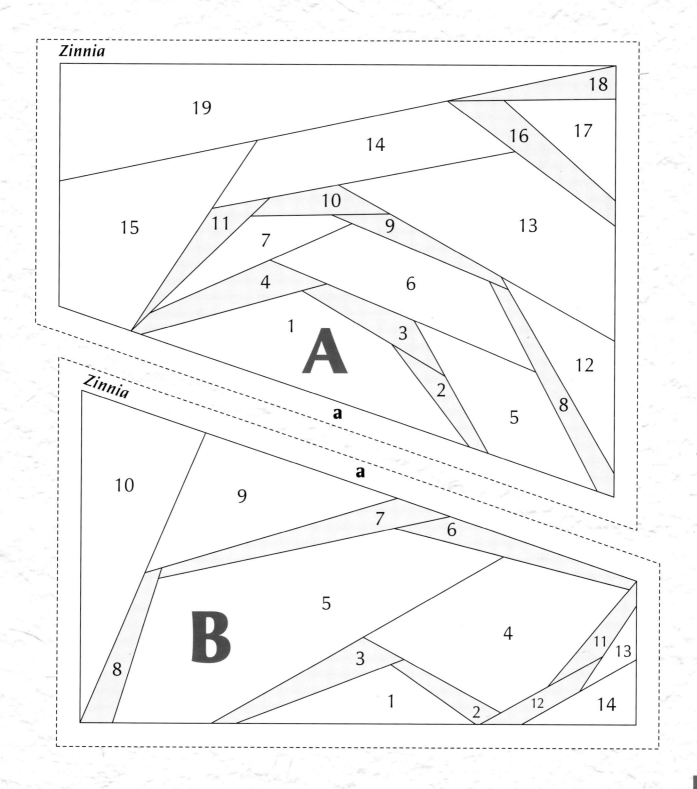

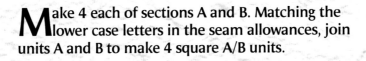

Center Medallion

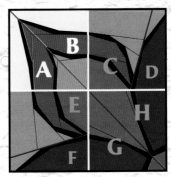

Make 4 each of sections A and B. Matching the lower case letters in the seam allowances, join units A and B to make 4 square A/B units.

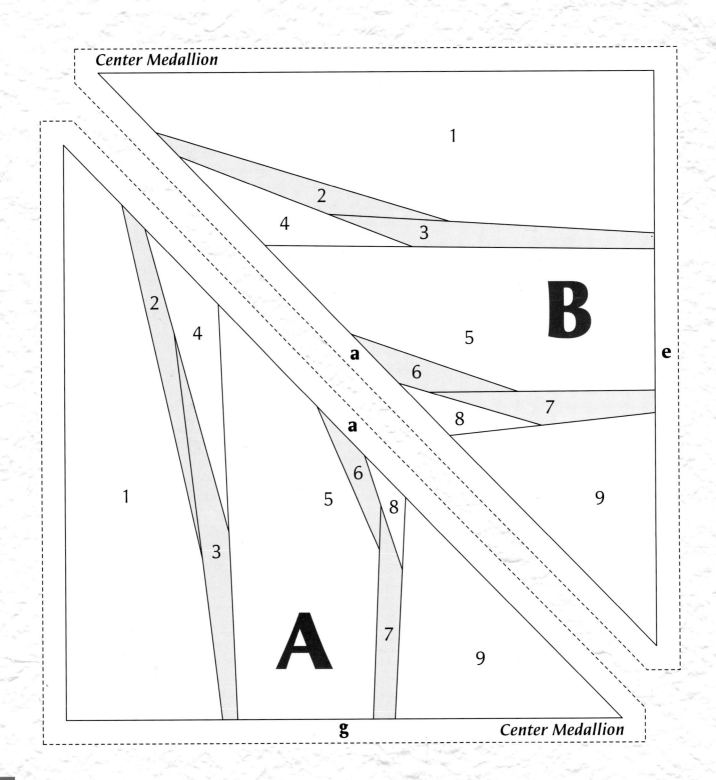

Center Medallion

B

1

2

4

3

5

a

6

7

8

a

e

5

6

8

9

A

1

2

4

3

7

9

g

Center Medallion

Center Medallion

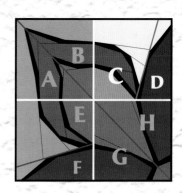

Make 4 each of sections C and D. Matching the lower case letters in the seam allowances, join units C and D to make 4 square C/D units.

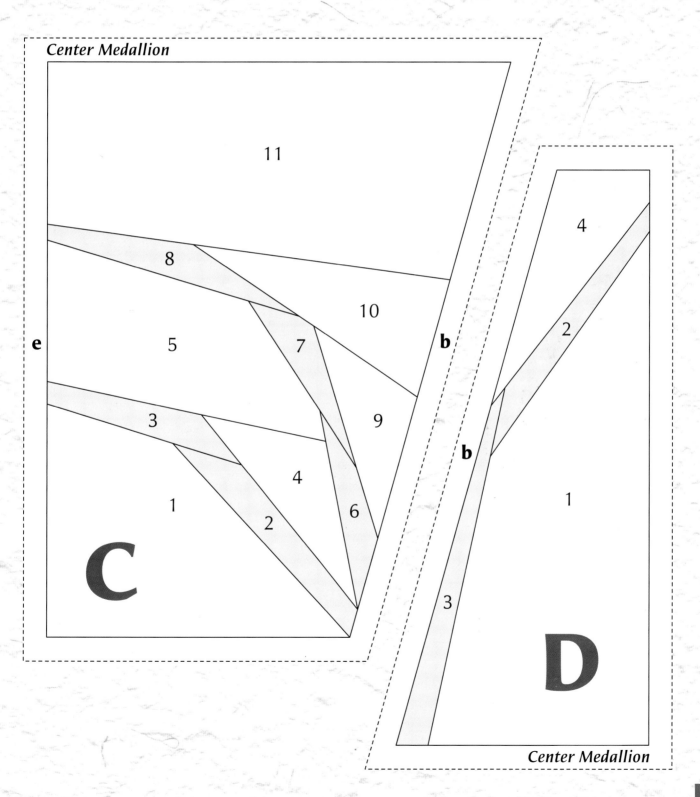

Center Medallion

11

8

10

e

5

7

3

4

1

2

6

9

b

b

4

2

1

3

C

D

Center Medallion

Center Medallion

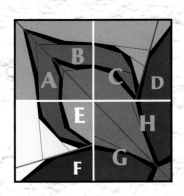

Make 4 each of sections E and F. Matching the lower case letters in the seam allowances, join units E and F to make 4 square E/F units.

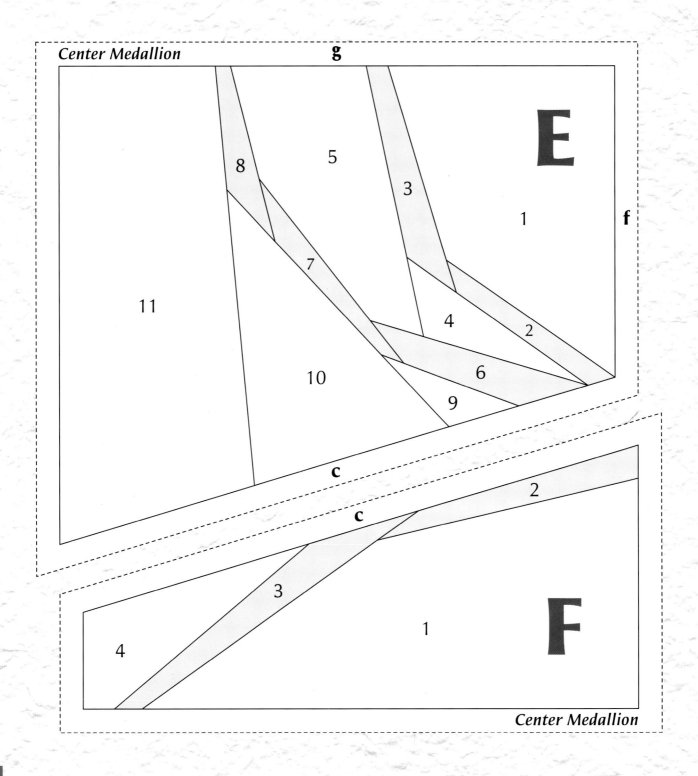

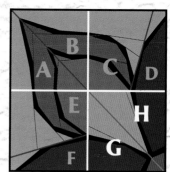

Center Medallion

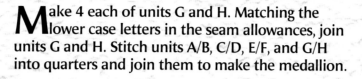

Make 4 each of units G and H. Matching the lower case letters in the seam allowances, join units G and H. Stitch units A/B, C/D, E/F, and G/H into quarters and join them to make the medallion.

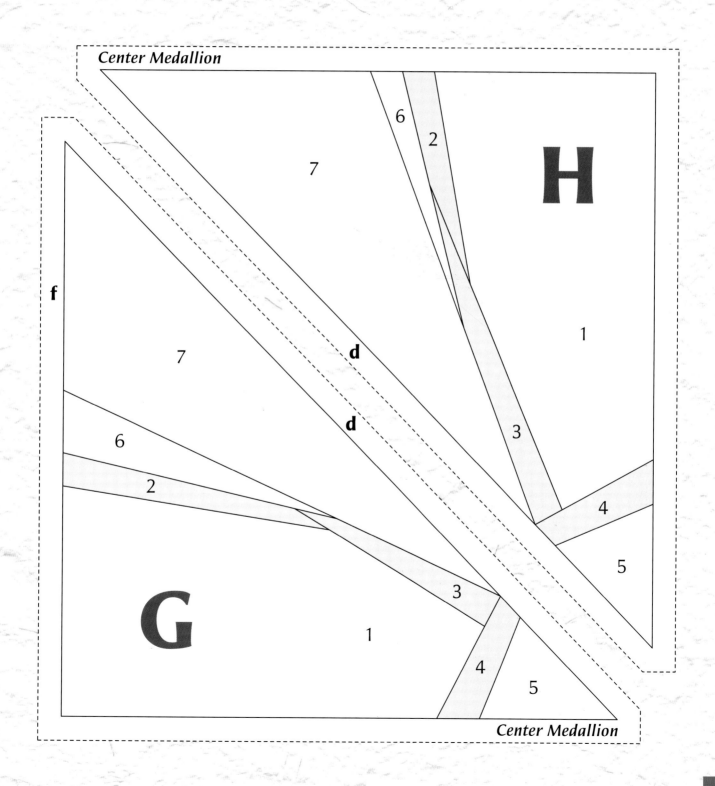

Center Medallion

H

6

2

7

f

d

d

1

3

6

2

4

5

G

7

3

1

4

5

Center Medallion

Leaves

Make 40 each of sections A and B. Set the completed units aside until the remaining blocks and sections are completed.

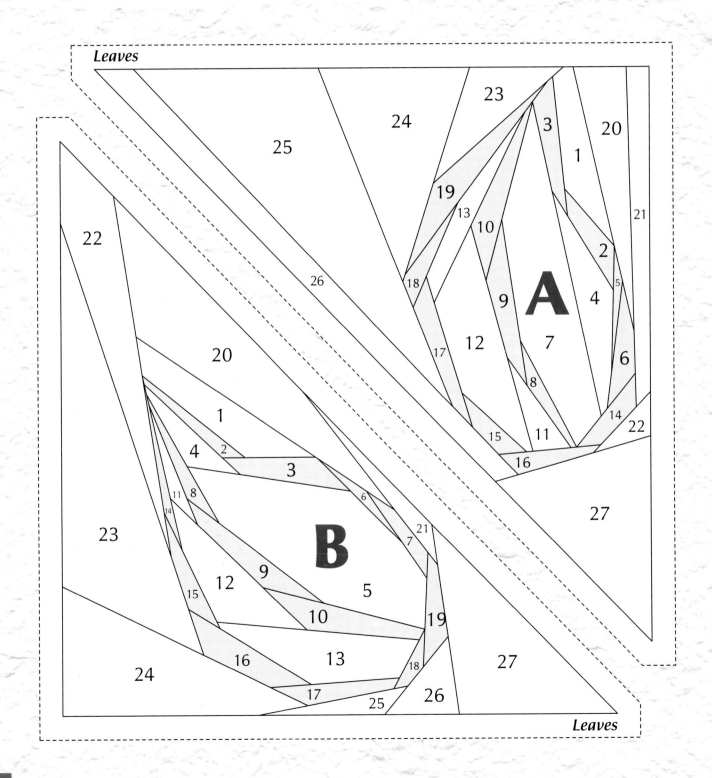

Leaves

25 24 23

3 20

1

19 13 10 2 21

22 18 9 A 4 5

26 12 7 6

20 17 8 14 22

1 15 11

4 2 16

3 6 27

11 8

14 B 21

23 9 7 5

12

15 19

10 27

16 13 18

24 17 25 26

Leaves

Border

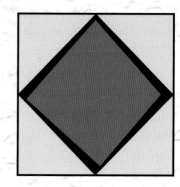

Make 36 of unit C using the orange and medium tan fabrics. Randomly placing scraps from the blocks, stitch 14 of Border unit A and 16 of Border unit B.

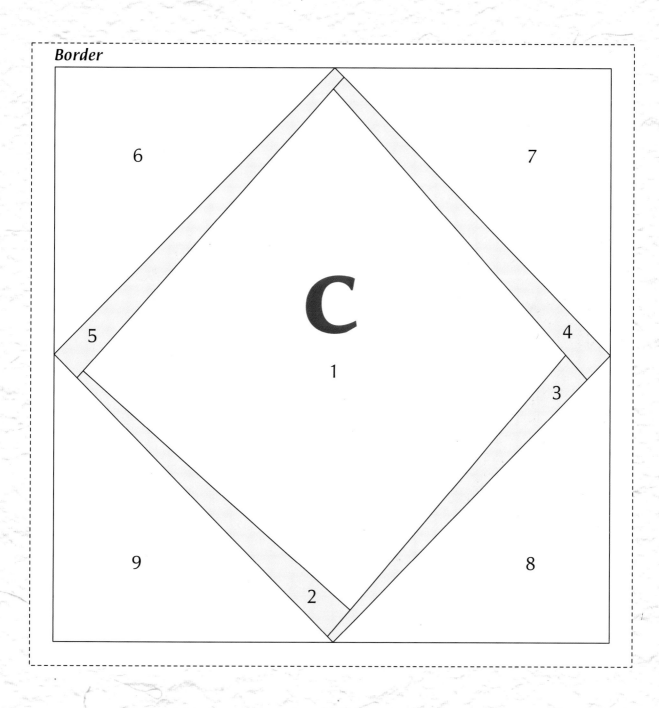

Border

6

7

5

C

4

1

3

9

8

2

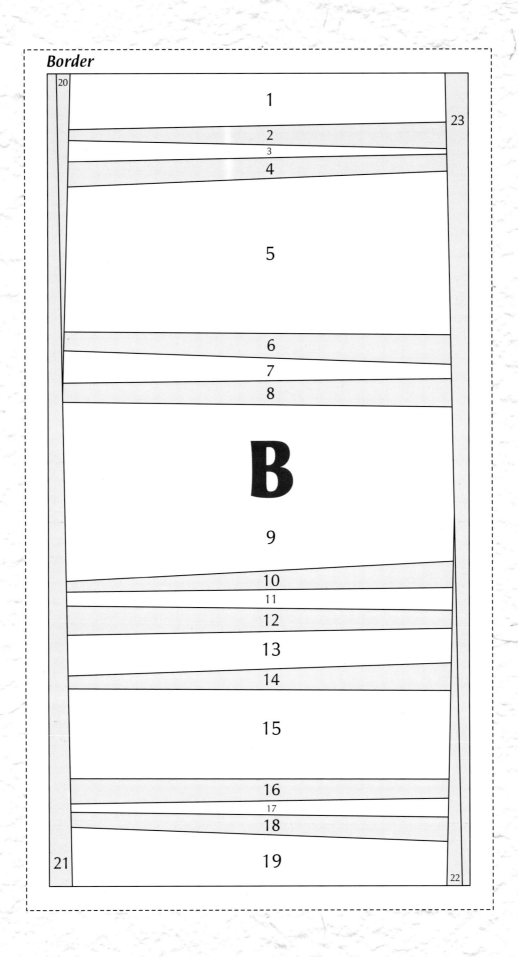

Border

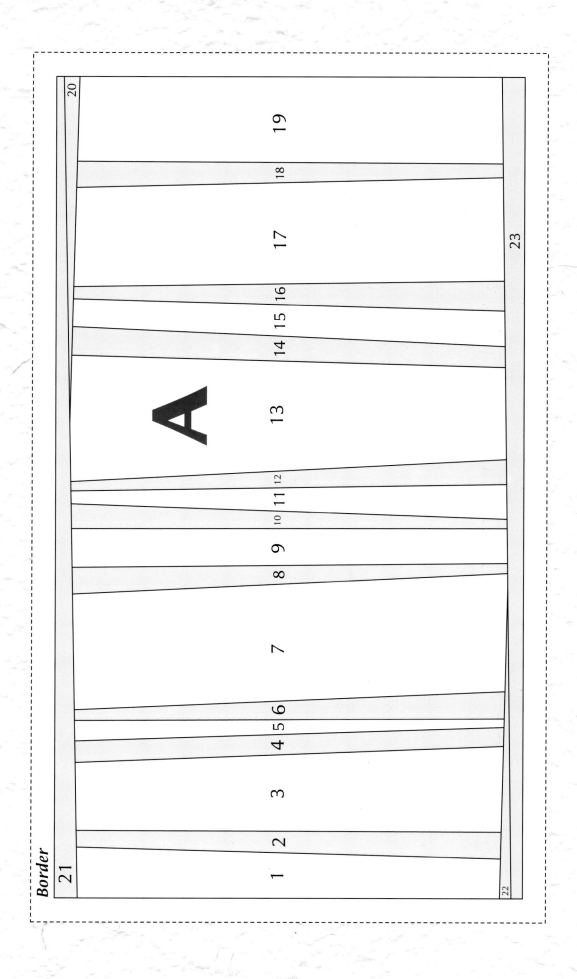

A few words
about the authors

Working together in 1995, Liz Schwartz and Stephen Seifert founded *The Foundation Piecer*, a quilting journal devoted to the art of foundation piecing. In addition to producing books and periodicals, they give lectures and conduct workshops on the foundation piecing technique. They are the authors of six best-selling books: *Birds of a Feather: A gathering of geese, Celestial Wonders: Foundation Pieced Stellar Designs, Foundation Pieced Stained Glass Quilts, Foundation Pieced Stained Glass Garden Stars, The Foundation Piecer: Volume 1,* and *Paper Piecing the Seasons,* as well as co-authors of *Foundation Pieced Nature Quilts.*

In her spare time, Liz enjoys making flameworked glass beads and Stephen enjoys spending time with family and photographing plants and flowers. Both Liz and Stephen live in the Blue Ridge mountains of Virginia with their son, Sebastian.

Available from Zippy Designs Publishing

Books

Birds of a Feather: A Gathering of Geese

Foundation Pieced Nature Quilts

Foundation Pieced Stained Glass Quilts

Foundation Pieced Stained Glass Garden Stars

The Foundation Piecer, Volume 1

Periodicals

The Foundation Piecer (quarterly pattern journal)

Tools

Add-A-Quarter Template Ruler

Easy Piece Foundation Paper

Paper Removal Tweezers

Wooden Seam Pressing Bar

Visit us on-line to download instructions to make California Breeze *(shown at right) as well as additional flower blocks to use with this book:*

www.zippydesigns.com